British Railways Pocket Book No. 4

18a £1.99

G000137968

THIRTIETH EDITION
2017

The Complete Guide to all
Electric Multiple Units which operate on
the national railway network

Robert Pritchard

ISBN 978 1909 431 33 1

© 2016. Platform 5 Publishing Ltd, 52 Broadfield Road, Sheffield, S8 0XJ, England.

Printed in England by The Lavenham Press, Lavenham, Suffolk.

CONTENTS

PROVISION OF INFORMATION

This book has been compiled with care to be as accurate as possible, but some information is not easily available and the publisher cannot be held responsible for any errors or omissions. We would like to thank the companies and individuals who have been helpful in supplying information to us. The authors of this series of books are always pleased to receive notification of any inaccuracies that may be found, to enhance future editions. Please send comments to:

Robert Pritchard, Platform 5 Publishing Ltd, 52 Broadfield Road, Sheffield, S8 0XJ, England.

e-mail: robert.pritchard@platform5.com   **Tel:** 0114 255 2625.

This book is updated to information received by 3 October 2016.

UPDATES

This book is updated to the Stock Changes given in **Today's Railways UK 179** (November 2016). The Platform 5 railway magazine "**Today's Railways UK**" publishes Stock Changes every month to update this book. The magazine also contains news and rolling stock information on the railways of Great Britain and Ireland and is published on the second Monday of every month. For further details of **Today's Railways UK**, please contact Platform 5 Publishing Ltd.

Front cover photograph: New 12-car Thameslink unit 700 110 is seen near Redhill with the 13.24 Bedford–Three Bridges on 22/08/16.   **Alex Dasi-Sutton**

BRITAIN'S RAILWAY SYSTEM

INFRASTRUCTURE & OPERATION

Britain's national railway infrastructure is owned by a "not for dividend" company, Network Rail. In 2014 Network Rail was reclassified as a public sector company, being described by the Government as a "public sector arm's-length body of the Department for Transport".

Most stations and maintenance depots are leased to and operated by Train Operating Companies (TOCs), but some larger stations are under Network Rail control. The only exception is the infrastructure on the Isle of Wight: The Island Line franchise uniquely included maintenance of the infrastructure as well as the operation of passenger services. As Island Line is now part of the South West Trains franchise, both the infrastructure and trains are operated by South West Trains.

Trains are operated by TOCs over Network Rail tracks (the National Network), regulated by access agreements between the parties involved. In general, TOCs are responsible for the provision and maintenance of the locomotives, rolling stock and staff necessary for the direct operation of services, whilst Network Rail is responsible for the provision and maintenance of the infrastructure and also for staff to regulate the operation of services.

The Department for Transport (DfT) is the franchising authority for the national network, with Transport Scotland overseeing the award of the ScotRail franchise and the Welsh Government overseeing the Wales & Borders franchise jointly with the DfT. TOCs can take commercial risks, although some franchises are "management contracts", where ticket revenues pass directly to the DfT. Concessions (such as London Overground) see the operator paid a fee to run the service, usually within tightly specified guidelines. Operators running a concession would not normally take commercial risks, although there are usually penalties and rewards in the contract.

During 2012 the letting of new franchises was suspended pending a review of the franchise system. The process restarted in 2013 but it is taking a number of years to catch-up and several franchises are receiving short-term extensions (or "Direct Awards") in the meantime.

DOMESTIC PASSENGER TRAIN OPERATORS

The majority of passenger trains are operated by TOCs on fixed-term franchises or concessions. Franchise expiry dates are shown in the list below:

Franchise	*Franchisee*	*Trading Name*
Caledonian Sleeper	Serco (until 31 March 2030)	**Caledonian Sleeper**

This new franchise started in April 2015 when operation of the ScotRail and ScotRail Sleeper franchises was separated. Abellio won the ScotRail franchise and Serco the Caledonian Sleeper franchise. Caledonian Sleeper operates four trains nightly between London Euston and Scotland using locomotives hired from GBRf or DB Schenker. New CAF rolling stock will be introduced from 2018.

Chiltern   Arriva (Deutsche Bahn)   **Chiltern Railways**
                                      (until 31 December 2021)

Chiltern Railways operates a frequent service between London Marylebone, Banbury and Birmingham Snow Hill, with some peak trains extending to Kidderminster. There are also regular services from Marylebone to Stratford-upon-Avon and to Aylesbury Vale Parkway via Amersham (along the London Underground Metropolitan Line). A new route to Oxford Parkway was added to the franchise in autumn 2015, and this line will be extended to Oxford in late 2016. The fleet consists of DMUs of Classes 121 (used on the Princes Risborough–Aylesbury route), 165, 168 and 172 plus a number of locomotive-hauled rakes used on some of the Birmingham route trains, worked by Class 68s hired from DRS.

Cross-Country   Arriva (Deutsche Bahn)   **CrossCountry**
                                      (until October 2019)
There is an option to extend the franchise by 1 year to October 2020.

CrossCountry operates a network of long distance services between Scotland, North-East England and Manchester to the South-West of England, Reading, Southampton, Bournemouth and Guildford, centred on Birmingham New Street. These trains are mainly formed of diesel Class 220/221 Voyagers, supplemented by a small number of HSTs on the NE–SW route. Inter-urban services also link Nottingham, Leicester and Stansted Airport with Birmingham and Cardiff. These use Class 170 DMUs.

Crossrail   MTR   **Crossrail**
                                      (until 30 May 2023)
There is an option to extend the concession by 2 years to May 2025.

This is a new concession which started in May 2015. Initially Crossrail took over the Liverpool Street–Shenfield stopping service from Abellio Greater Anglia, using a fleet of Class 315 EMUs, with the service branded "TfL Rail". New Class 345 EMUs will be introduced on this route from spring 2017 and then from 2018–19 Crossrail will operate through new tunnels beneath central London, from Shenfield and Abbey Wood in the east to Reading and Heathrow Airport in the west.

East Midlands   Stagecoach Group   **East Midlands Trains**
                                      (until 4 March 2018)
There is an option to extend the franchise by 1 year to March 2019.

EMT operates a mix of long distance high speed services on the Midland Main Line (MML), from London St Pancras to Sheffield (Leeds at peak times and some extensions to York/Scarborough) and Nottingham (plus peak-hour trains to Lincoln), and local and regional services ranging from the Norwich–Liverpool route to Nottingham–Skegness, Newark–Mansfield–Worksop, Nottingham–Matlock and Derby–Crewe. It also operates local services in Lincolnshire. Trains on the MML are worked by a fleet of Class 222 DMUs and nine HSTs, whilst the local and regional fleet consists of DMU Classes 153, 156 and 158.

Essex Thameside   National Express Group   **c2c**
                                      (until 8 November 2029)
There is an option to extend the franchise by seven reporting periods to May 2030.

c2c operates an intensive, principally commuter, service from London Fenchurch Street to Southend and Shoeburyness via both Upminster and Tilbury. The fleet consists entirely of Class 357 EMUs, with six Class 387s due to arrive in late 2016. In 2014 c2c won the new 15-year franchise that promised to introduce 17 new 4-car EMUs from 2019.

Greater Western
First Group
(until 1 April 2019)
Great Western Railway

There is an option to extend the franchise by 1 year to April 2020.

Great Western Railway (until September 2015 branded as First Great Western) operates long distance trains from London Paddington to South Wales, the West Country and Worcester and Hereford. In addition there are frequent trains along the Thames Valley corridor to Newbury/Bedwyn and Oxford, plus local and regional trains throughout the South-West including the Cornish, Devon and Thames Valley branches, the Reading–Gatwick North Downs line and Cardiff–Portsmouth Harbour and Bristol–Weymouth regional routes. A fleet of 54 HSTs is used on the long-distance trains, with DMUs of Classes 165 and 166 used on the North Downs and Thames Valley routes and Class 180s used alongside HSTs on the Cotswold Line to Worcester and Hereford. Classes 143, 150, 153 and 158 are used on local and regional trains in the South-West. A small fleet of four Class 57s is maintained to principally work the overnight "Cornish Riviera" Sleeper service between London Paddington and Penzance.

Greater Anglia
Abellio (Netherlands Railways)
(until 15 October 2025)
Abellio Greater Anglia

Abellio Greater Anglia operates main line trains between London Liverpool Street, Ipswich and Norwich and local trains across Norfolk, Suffolk and parts of Cambridgeshire. It also runs local and commuter services into London Liverpool Street from the Great Eastern (including Southend, Braintree and Clacton) and West Anglia (including Cambridge and Stansted Airport) routes. It operates a varied fleet of Class 90s with locomotive-hauled Mark 3 sets, DMUs of Classes 153, 156 and 170 and EMUs of Classes 317, 321, 360 and 379. Two locomotive-hauled sets, using Class 37s and 68s, are hired on a temporary basis for use on some trains between Norwich and Great Yarmouth/Lowestoft.

Integrated Kent
Govia (Go-Ahead/Keolis)
(until 24 June 2018)
Southeastern

Southeastern operates all services in the South-East London suburbs, the whole of Kent and part of Sussex, which are primarily commuter services to London. It also operates domestic high speed trains on HS1 from London St Pancras to Ashford, Ramsgate, Dover and Faversham with additional peak services on other routes. EMUs of Classes 375, 376, 465 and 466 are used, along with Class 395s on the High Speed trains.

InterCity East Coast
Stagecoach/Virgin Trains
(until 31 March 2023)
Virgin Trains East Coast

There is an option to extend the franchise by 1 year to March 2024.

Virgin Trains East Coast operates frequent long distance trains on the East Coast Main Line between London King's Cross, Leeds, York, Newcastle and Edinburgh, with less frequent services to Bradford, Harrogate, Skipton, Hull, Lincoln, Glasgow, Aberdeen and Inverness. A mixed fleet of Class 91s and 30 Mark 4 sets, and 15 HST sets, are used on these trains.

InterCity West Coast
Virgin Rail Group (Virgin/Stagecoach Group)
(until 31 March 2018)
Virgin Trains

Virgin Trains operates long distance services along the West Coast Main Line from London Euston to Birmingham/Wolverhampton, Manchester, Liverpool and Glasgow using Class 390 Pendolino EMUs. It also operates Class 221 Voyagers on the Euston–Chester–Holyhead route, whilst a mixture of 221s and 390s are used on the Euston–Birmingham–Glasgow/Edinburgh route.

London Rail   MTR/Arriva (Deutsche Bahn)   **London Overground**
(until 12 November 2016)

This is a Concession and is different from other rail franchises, as fares and service levels are set by Transport for London instead of by the DfT.

London Overground operates services on the Richmond–Stratford North London Line and the Willesden Junction–Clapham Junction West London Line, plus the East London Line from Highbury & Islington to New Cross and New Cross Gate, with extensions to Clapham Jn (via Denmark Hill), Crystal Palace and West Croydon. It also runs services from London Euston to Watford Junction. All these use Class 378 EMUs whilst Class 172 DMUs are used on the Gospel Oak–Barking route. London Overground also took over the operation of some suburban services from London Liverpool Street in 2015 – to Chingford, Enfield Town and Cheshunt. These use Class 315 and 317 EMUs.

Merseyrail Electrics   Serco/Abellio (Netherlands Railways)   **Merseyrail**
(until 19 July 2028)

Under the control of Merseytravel PTE instead of the DfT. Franchise reviewed every five years to fit in with the Merseyside Local Transport Plan.

Merseyrail operates services between Liverpool and Southport, Ormskirk, Kirkby, Hunts Cross, New Brighton, West Kirby, Chester and Ellesmere Port, using Class 507 and 508 EMUs.

Northern Rail   Arriva (Deutsche Bahn)   **Northern**
(until 31 March 2025)

There is an option to extend the franchise by 1 year to March 2026.

Northern, operated by Arriva since April 2016, operates a range of inter-urban, commuter and rural services throughout the North of England, including those around the cities of Leeds, Manchester, Sheffield, Liverpool and Newcastle. The network extends from Chathill in the north to Nottingham in the south, and Cleethorpes in the east to St Bees in the west. Long distance services include Leeds–Carlisle, Middlesbrough–Carlisle and York–Blackpool North. The operator uses a large fleet of DMUs of Classes 142, 144, 150, 153, 155, 156 and 158 plus EMU Classes 319, 321, 322, 323 and 333. Class 185s are hired from TransPennine Express for use on some services between Manchester Airport and Blackpool North/Barrow/Windermere. Two locomotive-hauled sets, with Class 37s, are hired from DRS for use on some trains between Carlisle and Barrow-in-Furness/Preston.

ScotRail   Abellio (Netherlands Railways)   **ScotRail**
(until 31 March 2022)

There is an option to extend the franchise by 3 years to March 2025.

ScotRail provides almost all passenger services within Scotland and also trains from Glasgow to Carlisle via Dumfries, some of which extend to Newcastle (jointly operated with Northern). The company operates a large fleet of DMUs of Classes 156, 158 and 170 and EMU Classes 314, 318, 320, 334 and 380. Two locomotive-hauled rakes are also used on Fife Circle commuter trains, hauled by Class 68s hired from DRS.

South Western   Stagecoach Group   **South West Trains**
(until June 2017)

South West Trains operates trains from London Waterloo to destinations across the South and South-West including Woking, Basingstoke, Southampton, Portsmouth, Salisbury, Exeter, Reading and Weymouth as well as suburban services from Waterloo. SWT also runs services between Ryde and Shanklin on the Isle of Wight, using former London Underground 1938 stock (Class 483s). The rest of the fleet consists of DMU Classes 158 and 159 and EMU Classes 444, 450, 455, 456 and 458. Class 707s will be introduced in 2017.

Thameslink & Great Northern   Govia (Go-Ahead/Keolis)   **Govia Thameslink Railway**
(until 19 September 2021)
There is an option to extend the franchise by 2 years to September 2023.

Govia operates this franchise, the largest in the UK, as a management contract. The former Southern franchise was combined with Thameslink/Great Northern in 2015. GTR uses four brands within the franchise: "Thameslink" for trains between Bedford and Brighton via central London and also on the Sutton/Wimbledon loop using Class 319, 377, 387 and new 700 EMUs. Some trains continue into Southeastern territory to Sevenoaks, Orpington and Ashford. "Great Northern" comprises services from London King's Cross and Moorgate to Welwyn Garden City, Hertford North, Peterborough, Cambridge and Kings Lynn using Class 313, 317, 321, 365 and 387 EMUs. "Southern" operates predominantly commuter services between London, Surrey and Sussex and metro services in South London, as well as services along the South Coast between Southampton, Brighton, Hastings and Ashford, plus the cross-London service from South Croydon to Milton Keynes. Class 171 DMUs are used on Brighton–Ashford and London Bridge–Uckfield services, whilst all other services are in the hands of Class 313, 377 and 455 EMUs. Finally, the premium "Gatwick Express" operates non-stop trains between London Victoria, Gatwick Airport and Brighton using Class 387/2 EMUs.

Trans-Pennine Express   First Group/Keolis   **TransPennine Express**
(until 31 March 2023)
There is an option to extend the franchise by 2 years to March 2025.

TransPennine Express operates predominantly long distance inter-urban services linking major cities across the North of England, along with Edinburgh and Glasgow in Scotland. The main services are Manchester Airport/Manchester Piccadilly–Newcastle/Middlesbrough/ Hull plus Liverpool–Scarborough and Liverpool–Newcastle along the North Trans-Pennine route via Huddersfield, Leeds and York, and Manchester Airport–Cleethorpes along the South Trans-Pennine route via Sheffield. TPE also operates Manchester Airport–Edinburgh/Glasgow. Services to Blackpool North/Barrow/Windermere are now operated by Northern, The fleet consists of Class 185 DMUs, plus Class 350 EMUs used on Manchester Airport–Scotland services.

Wales & Borders   Arriva (Deutsche Bahn)   **Arriva Trains Wales**
(until 14 October 2018)
The franchise agreement includes the provision for the term to be further extended by mutual agreement by up to five years beyond October 2018. Management of the franchise is devolved to the Welsh Government, but DfT is still the procuring authority.

Arriva Trains Wales operates a mix of long distance, regional and local services throughout Wales, including the Valley Lines network of lines around Cardiff, and also through services to the English border counties and to Manchester and Birmingham. The fleet consists of DMUs of Classes 142, 143, 150, 158 and 175 and two loco-hauled rakes: one used on a premium Welsh Government sponsored service on the Cardiff–Holyhead route, and one used between Manchester/Crewe and Holyhead (both are hauled by a Class 67).

West Midlands   Govia (Go-Ahead/Keolis)   **London Midland**
(until October 2017)

London Midland operates long distance and regional services from London Euston to Northampton and Birmingham/Crewe and also between Birmingham and Liverpool as well as local and regional services around Birmingham, including to Stratford-upon-Avon, Worcester, Hereford, Redditch and Shrewsbury. It also operates the Bedford–Bletchley and Watford Jn–St Albans Abbey branches. The fleet consists of DMU Classes 150, 153, 170 and 172 and EMU Classes 319, 323 and 350.

The following operators run non-franchised services (* special summer services only):

Operator	Trading Name	Route
BAA	Heathrow Express	London Paddington–Heathrow Airport
Hull Trains (part of First)	Hull Trains	London King's Cross–Hull
Grand Central (part of Arriva)	Grand Central	London King's Cross–Sunderland/ Bradford Interchange
North Yorkshire Moors Railway Enterprises	North Yorkshire Moors Railway	Pickering–Grosmont–Whitby/ Battersby
West Coast Railway Company	West Coast Railway Company	Birmingham–Stratford-upon-Avon* Fort William–Mallaig* York–Settle–Carlisle*

INTERNATIONAL PASSENGER OPERATORS

Eurostar International operates passenger services between the UK and mainland Europe. The company, established in 2010, is jointly owned by SNCF (the national operator of France): 55%, SNCB (the national operator of Belgium): 5% and Patina Rail: 40%. Patina Rail is made up of Canadian-based Caisse de dépôt et placement du Québec (CDPG) and UK-based Hermes Infrastructure (owning 30% and 10% respectively). This 40% was previously owned by the UK Government until it was sold in 2015.

In addition, a service for the conveyance of accompanied road vehicles through the Channel Tunnel is provided by the tunnel operating company, Eurotunnel.

INTRODUCTION

This book contains details of all Electric Multiple Units, usually referred to as EMUs, which can run on Britain's national railway network.

The number of EMUs in operation has been steadily increasing in recent years as both more lines have been opened or have been electrified and as the number of passengers travelling on the network has increased. EMUs work a wide variety of services, from long distance Intercity (such as the Class 390 Pendolinos) to inter-urban and suburban duties.

LAYOUT OF INFORMATION

25 kV AC 50 Hz overhead EMUs and dual voltage EMUs are listed in numerical order of set numbers. Individual "loose" vehicles are listed in numerical order after vehicles formed into fixed formations.

750 V DC third rail EMUs are listed in numerical order of class number, then in numerical order of set number. Some of these use the former Southern Region four-digit set numbers. These are derived from theoretical six digit set numbers which are the four-digit set number prefixed by the first two numbers of the class.

Where sets or vehicles have been renumbered in recent years, former numbering detail is shown alongside current detail. Each entry is laid out as in the following example:

Set No.	Detail	Livery	Owner	Operator	Allocation	Formation
5912	†	**SS**	P	*SW*	WD	77835 62837 67400 77836

Codes: Codes are used to denote the livery, owner, operator and depot allocation of each Electric Multiple Unit. Details of these can be found in section 9 of this book. Where a unit or spare car is off-lease, the operator column is left blank.

Detail Differences: Detail differences which currently affect the areas and types of train which vehicles may work are shown, plus differences in interior layout. Where such differences occur within a class, these are shown either in the heading information or alongside the individual set or vehicle number.

Set Formations: Regular set formations are shown where these are normally maintained. Readers should note set formations might be temporarily varied from time to time to suit maintenance and/or operational requirements. Vehicles shown as "Spare" are not formed in any regular set formation.

Names: Only names carried with official sanction are listed. Names are shown in UPPER/lower case characters as actually shown on the name carried on the vehicle(s). Unless otherwise shown, complete units are regarded as named rather than just the individual car(s) which carry the name.

GENERAL INFORMATION

CLASSIFICATION AND NUMBERING

25 kV AC 50 Hz overhead and "Versatile" EMUs are classified in the series 300–399. 750 V DC third rail EMUs are classified in the series 400–599. More recently dual-voltage units have been numbered in the 700–710 series.

Until 2014 EMU individual cars were numbered in the series 61000–78999, except for vehicles used on the Isle of Wight – which are numbered in a separate series, and the Class 378s, 380s and 395s, which took up the 38xxx and 39xxx series'.

For all new vehicles allocated by the Rolling Stock Library since 2014 6-digit vehicle numbers have been used. So far this applies to Classes 345, 385, 387, 700, 707, 800 and 801.

Any vehicle constructed or converted to replace another vehicle following accident damage and carrying the same number as the original vehicle is denoted by the suffix[II] in this publication.

UNITS OF MEASUREMENT

Principal details and dimensions are quoted for each class in metric and/or imperial units as considered appropriate bearing in mind common UK usage.

All dimensions and weights are quoted for vehicles in an "as new" condition with all necessary supplies (eg oil, water, sand) on board. Dimensions are quoted in the order Length – Width. All lengths quoted are over buffers or couplers as appropriate. Where two lengths are quoted, the first refers to outer vehicles in a set and the second to inner vehicles. All width dimensions quoted are maxima. All weights are shown as metric tonnes (t = tonnes).

Bogie Types are quoted in the format motored/non-motored (eg BP20/BT13 denotes BP20 motored bogies and BT non-motored bogies).

Unless noted to the contrary, all vehicles listed have bar couplers at non-driving ends.

Traction motors power details refer to each motored car per unit.

Vehicles ordered under the auspices of BR were allocated a Lot (batch) number when ordered and these are quoted in class headings and sub-headings. Vehicles ordered since 1995 have no Lot Numbers, but the manufacturer and location that they were built are given.

OPERATING CODES

These codes are used by train operating company staff to describe the various different types of vehicles and normally appear on data panels on the inner (ie non driving) ends of vehicles.

A "B" prefix indicates a battery vehicle.

A "P" prefix indicates a trailer vehicle on which is mounted the pantograph, instead of the default case where the pantograph is mounted on a motor vehicle.

The first part of the code describes whether or not the car has a motor or a driving cab as follows:

DM	Driving motor	M	Motor	T Trailer
DT	Driving trailer			

The next letter is a "B" for cars with a brake compartment.
This is followed by the saloon details:

F	First	S	Standard	C Composite

The next letter denotes the style of accommodation, which is "O" for Open for all EMU vehicles still in service.

Finally vehicles with a buffet or kitchen area are suffixed RB or RMB for a miniature buffet counter.

Where two vehicles of the same type are formed within the same unit, the above codes may be suffixed by (A) and (B) to differentiate between vehicles.

A composite is a vehicle containing both First and Standard Class accommodation, whilst a brake vehicle is a vehicle containing separate specific accommodation for the conductor.

ACCOMMODATION

The information given in class headings and sub-headings is in the form F/S nT (or TD) nW. For example 12/54 1T 1W denotes 12 First Class and 54 Standard Class seats, one toilet and one space for a wheelchair. A number in brackets (ie (+2)) denotes tip-up seats (in addition to the fixed seats). Tip-up seats in vestibules do not count. The seating layout of open saloons is shown as 2+1, 2+2 or 3+2 as the case may be. Where units have First Class accommodation as well as Standard Class and the layout is different for each class then these are shown separately prefixed by "1:" and "2:". TD denotes a toilet suitable for use by a disabled person.

ABBREVIATIONS

The following standard abbreviations are used in class headings and also throughout this publication:

AC	Alternating Current.	kW	kilowatts.
BR	British Railways.	LT	London Transport.
BSI	Bergische Stahl Industrie.	LUL	London Underground Limited.
DC	Direct Current.	m	metres.
EMU	Electric Multiple Unit.	mph	miles per hour.
Hz	Hertz.	SR	BR Southern Region.
kN	kilonewtons.	V	volts.
km/h	kilometres per hour.		

NEW EMUS ON ORDER

Where possible all EMUs for which firm orders have been placed are listed in this book. However there are a number of new EMUs that are on order but for which the unit number and/or vehicle number series' have not yet been confirmed. These are summarised in the table below:

Class	Manufacturer	Operator	Quantity	Delivery dates
331	CAF	Northern	31 x 3-car	2017–19
331	CAF	Northern	12 x 4-car	2017–19
397	CAF	TransPennine Express	12 x 5-car	2019
710/1	Bombardier	Ldn Overground (AC)	31 x 4-car[1]	2017–18
710/2	Bombardier	Ldn Overground (AC/DC)	14 x 4-car[1]	2017–18
717	Siemens	Govia Thameslink (GN)	25 x 6-car	2018–19
802/0	Hitachi	GWR (bi-mode)	22 x 5-car[2]	2018
802/1	Hitachi	GWR (bi-mode)	14 x 9-car[2]	2018
802/2	Hitachi	TP Express (bi-mode)	19 x 5-car	2019–20
tbc	Stadler	Greater Anglia	20 x 12-car	2019
tbc	Stadler	Greater Anglia (bi-mode)	14 x 3-car	2019
tbc	Stadler	Greater Anglia (bi-mode)	24 x 4-car	2019
tbc	Bombardier	Greater Anglia	22 x 10-car	2020
tbc	Bombardier	Greater Anglia	89 x 5-car	2020

[1] There is an option for up to a further 249 Class 710 vehicles.
[2] There is an option for up to 87 more vehicles.

1. 25 kV AC 50 Hz OVERHEAD & DUAL VOLTAGE UNITS

Except where otherwise stated, all units in this section operate on 25 kV AC 50 Hz overhead only.

CLASS 313   BREL YORK

Inner suburban units.

Formation: DMSO–PTSO–BDMSO or DMSO–TSO–BDMSO.
Systems: 25 kV AC overhead/750 V DC third rail.
Construction: Steel underframe, aluminium alloy body and roof.
Traction Motors: Four GEC G310AZ of 82.125 kW.
Wheel Arrangement: Bo-Bo + 2-2 + Bo-Bo.
Braking: Disc & rheostatic.   **Dimensions:** 20.33/20.18 x 2.82 m.
Bogies: BX1.   **Couplers:** Tightlock.
Gangways: Within unit + end doors.   **Control System:** Camshaft.
Doors: Sliding.   **Maximum Speed:** 75 mph.
Seating Layout: Various, see sub-class headings.
Multiple Working: Within class.

DMSO. Lot No. 30879 1976–77. –/74. 36.0 t.
PTSO. Lot No. 30880 1976–77. –/83. 31.0 t.
BDMSO. Lot No. 30885 1976–77. –/74. 37.5 t.

Class 313/0. Standard Design. Refurbished with high back seating (3+2 facing).

313 018	**FU**	E	*GN*	HE	62546	71230	62610
313 024	**FU**	E	*GN*	HE	62552	71236	62616
313 025	**FU**	E	*GN*	HE	62553	71237	62617
313 026	**FU**	E	*GN*	HE	62554	71238	62618
313 027	**FU**	E	*GN*	HE	62555	71239	62619
313 028	**FU**	E	*GN*	HE	62556	71240	62620
313 029	**FU**	E	*GN*	HE	62557	71241	62621
313 030	**FU**	E	*GN*	HE	62558	71242	62622
313 031	**FU**	E	*GN*	HE	62559	71243	62623
313 032	**FU**	E	*GN*	HE	62560	71244	62643
313 033	**FU**	E	*GN*	HE	62561	71245	62625
313 035	**FU**	E	*GN*	HE	62563	71247	62627
313 036	**FU**	E	*GN*	HE	62564	71248	62628
313 037	**FU**	E	*GN*	HE	62565	71249	62629
313 038	**FU**	E	*GN*	HE	62566	71250	62630
313 039	**FU**	E	*GN*	HE	62567	71251	62631
313 040	**FU**	E	*GN*	HE	62568	71252	62632
313 041	**FU**	E	*GN*	HE	62569	71253	62633
313 042	**FU**	E	*GN*	HE	62570	71254	62634
313 043	**FU**	E	*GN*	HE	62571	71255	62635
313 044	**FU**	E	*GN*	HE	62572	71256	62636
313 045	**FU**	E	*GN*	HE	62573	71257	62637
313 046	**FU**	E	*GN*	HE	62574	71258	62638

313047	**FU**	E	*GN*	HE	62575	71259	62639
313048	**FU**	E	*GN*	HE	62576	71260	62640
313049	**FU**	E	*GN*	HE	62577	71261	62641
313050	**FU**	E	*GN*	HE	62578	71262	62649
313051	**FU**	E	*GN*	HE	62579	71263	62624
313052	**FU**	E	*GN*	HE	62580	71264	62644
313053	**FU**	E	*GN*	HE	62581	71265	62645
313054	**FU**	E	*GN*	HE	62582	71266	62646
313055	**FU**	E	*GN*	HE	62583	71267	62647
313056	**FU**	E	*GN*	HE	62584	71268	62648
313057	**FU**	E	*GN*	HE	62585	71269	62642
313058	**FU**	E	*GN*	HE	62586	71270	62650
313059	**FU**	E	*GN*	HE	62587	71271	62651
313060	**FU**	E	*GN*	HE	62588	71272	62652
313061	**FU**	E	*GN*	HE	62589	71273	62653
313062	**FU**	E	*GN*	HE	62590	71274	62654
313063	**FU**	E	*GN*	HE	62591	71275	62655
313064	**FU**	E	*GN*	HE	62592	71276	62656

Name (carried on PTSO): 313054   Captain William Leefe Robinson V.C.

Class 313/1. Former London Overground units. Original low back seating (3+2 facing). Details as Class 313/0.

313122	**FU**	E	*GN*	HE	62550	71234	62614
313123	**FU**	E	*GN*	HE	62551	71235	62615
313134	**FU**	E	*GN*	HE	62562	71246	62626

Names (carried on PTSO):

313122   Eric Roberts 1946–2012 "The Flying Nottsman"
313134   City of London

Class 313/2. Southern units. Units refurbished for Southern for Brighton Coastway services. Fitted with 2+2 mainly facing high-back seating. 750 V DC only (pantographs removed).

DMSO. Lot No. 30879 1976–77. –/64. 37.0 t.
TSO. Lot No. 30880 1976–77. –/64(+2). 31.0 t.
BDMSO. Lot No. 30885 1976–77. –/64. 37.0 t.

313201	(313101)	**SN**	BN	*SN*	BI	62529	71213	62593
313202	(313102)	**SN**	BN	*SN*	BI	62530	71214	62594
313203	(313103)	**SN**	BN	*SN*	BI	62531	71215	62595
313204	(313104)	**SN**	BN	*SN*	BI	62532	71216	62596
313205	(313105)	**SN**	BN	*SN*	BI	62533	71217	62597
313206	(313106)	**SN**	BN	*SN*	BI	62534	71218	62598
313207	(313107)	**SN**	BN	*SN*	BI	62535	71219	62599
313208	(313108)	**SN**	BN	*SN*	BI	62536	71220	62600
313209	(313109)	**SN**	BN	*SN*	BI	62537	71221	62601
313210	(313110)	**SN**	BN	*SN*	BI	62538	71222	62602
313211	(313111)	**SN**	BN	*SN*	BI	62539	71223	62603
313212	(313112)	**SN**	BN	*SN*	BI	62540	71224	62604
313213	(313113)	**SN**	BN	*SN*	BI	62541	71225	62605
313214	(313114)	**SN**	BN	*SN*	BI	62542	71226	62606

313215	(313115)	**SN**	BN	*SN*	BI	62543	71227	62607
313216	(313116)	**SN**	BN	*SN*	BI	62544	71228	62608
313217	(313117)	**SN**	BN	*SN*	BI	62545	71229	62609
313219	(313119)	**SN**	BN	*SN*	BI	62547	71231	62611
313220	(313120)	**SN**	BN	*SN*	BI	62548	71232	62612

CLASS 314   BREL YORK

Inner suburban units.

Formation: DMSO–PTSO–DMSO.
Construction: Steel underframe, aluminium alloy body and roof.
Traction Motors: Four GEC G310AZ (* Brush TM61-53) of 82.125 kW.
Wheel Arrangement: Bo-Bo + 2-2 + Bo-Bo.
Braking: Disc & rheostatic.   **Dimensions:** 20.33/20.18 x 2.82 m.
Bogies: BX1.   **Couplers:** Tightlock.
Gangways: Within unit + end doors. **Control System:** Thyristor.
Doors: Sliding.   **Maximum Speed:** 70 mph.
Seating Layout: 3+2 low-back facing.
Multiple Working: Within class and with Class 315.

DMSO. Lot No. 30912 1979. –/68. 34.5 t.
64588II. **DMSO.** Lot No. 30908 1978–80. Rebuilt Railcare Glasgow 1996 from
Class 507 No. 64426. The original 64588 was scrapped. –/74. 34.5 t.
PTSO. Lot No. 30913 1979. –/76. 33.0 t.

314201	*	**SC**	A	*SR*	GW	64583	71450	64584
314202	*	**SC**	A	*SR*	GW	64585	71451	64586
314203	*	**SR**	A	*SR*	GW	64587	71452	64588II
314204	*	**SR**	A	*SR*	GW	64589	71453	64590
314205	*	**SC**	A	*SR*	GW	64591	71454	64592
314206	*	**SC**	A	*SR*	GW	64593	71455	64594
314207		**SC**	A	*SR*	GW	64595	71456	64596
314208		**SR**	A	*SR*	GW	64597	71457	64598
314209		**SC**	A	*SR*	GW	64599	71458	64600
314210		**SC**	A	*SR*	GW	64601	71459	64602
314211		**SR**	A	*SR*	GW	64603	71460	64604
314212		**SR**	A	*SR*	GW	64605	71461	64606
314213		**SC**	A	*SR*	GW	64607	71462	64608
314214		**SC**	A	*SR*	GW	64609	71463	64610
314215		**SC**	A	*SR*	GW	64611	71464	64612
314216		**SC**	A	*SR*	GW	64613	71465	64614

CLASS 315   BREL YORK

Inner suburban units.

Formation: DMSO–TSO–PTSO–DMSO.
Construction: Steel underframe, aluminium alloy body and roof.
Traction Motors: Four Brush TM61-53 (* GEC G310AZ) of 82.125 kW.
Wheel Arrangement: Bo-Bo + 2-2 + 2-2 + Bo-Bo.
Braking: Disc & rheostatic.   **Dimensions:** 20.18 x 2.82 m.
Bogies: BX1.   **Couplers:** Tightlock.

Gangways: Within unit + end doors. **Control System:** Thyristor.
Doors: Sliding.   **Maximum Speed:** 75 mph.
Seating Layout: 3+2 low-back facing.
Multiple Working: Within class and with Class 314.

DMSO. Lot No. 30902 1980–81. –/74. 38.2 t.
TSO. Lot No. 30904 1980–81. –/86. 27.4 t.
PTSO. Lot No. 30903 1980–81. –/75(+7) 2W. 33.8 t.

315801		LO	E	LO	IL	64461	71281	71389	64462
315802		LO	E	LO	IL	64463	71282	71390	64464
315803		LO	E	LO	IL	64465	71283	71391	64466
315804		LO	E	LO	IL	64467	71284	71392	64468
315805		LO	E	LO	IL	64469	71285	71393	64470
315806		LO	E	LO	IL	64471	71286	71394	64472
315807		LO	E	LO	IL	64473	71287	71395	64474
315808		LO	E	LO	IL	64475	71288	71396	64476
315809		LO	E	LO	IL	64477	71289	71397	64478
315810		LO	E	LO	IL	64479	71290	71398	64480
315811		LO	E	LO	IL	64481	71291	71399	64482
315812		LO	E	LO	IL	64483	71292	71400	64484
315813		LO	E	LO	IL	64485	71293	71401	64486
315814		LO	E	LO	IL	64487	71294	71402	64488
315815		LO	E	LO	IL	64489	71295	71403	64490
315816		LO	E	LO	IL	64491	71296	71404	64492
315817		LO	E	LO	IL	64493	71297	71405	64494
315818		XR	E	XR	IL	64495	71298	71406	64496
315819		XR	E	XR	IL	64497	71299	71407	64498
315820		XR	E	XR	IL	64499	71300	71408	64500
315821		XR	E	XR	IL	64501	71301	71409	64502
315822		XR	E	XR	IL	64503	71302	71410	64504
315823		XR	E	XR	IL	64505	71303	71411	64506
315824		XR	E	XR	IL	64507	71304	71412	64508
315825		XR	E	XR	IL	64509	71305	71413	64510
315826		XR	E	XR	IL	64511	71306	71414	64512
315827		XR	E	XR	IL	64513	71307	71415	64514
315828		XR	E	XR	IL	64515	71308	71416	64516
315829		XR	E	XR	IL	64517	71309	71417	64518
315830		XR	E	XR	IL	64519	71310	71418	64520
315831		XR	E	XR	IL	64521	71311	71419	64522
315832		XR	E	XR	IL	64523	71312	71420	64524
315833		XR	E	XR	IL	64525	71313	71421	64526
315834		XR	E	XR	IL	64527	71314	71422	64528
315835		XR	E	XR	IL	64529	71315	71423	64530
315836		XR	E	XR	IL	64531	71316	71424	64532
315837		XR	E	XR	IL	64533	71317	71425	64534
315838		XR	E	XR	IL	64535	71318	71426	64536
315839		XR	E	XR	IL	64537	71319	71427	64538
315840		XR	E	XR	IL	64539	71320	71428	64540
315841		XR	E	XR	IL	64541	71321	71429	64542
315842	*	XR	E	XR	IL	64543	71322	71430	64544
315843	*	XR	E	XR	IL	64545	71323	71431	64546

315844	*	**XR**	E	*XR*	IL	64547	71324	71432	64548
315845	*	**XR**	E	*XR*	IL	64549	71325	71433	64550
315846	*	**XR**	E	*XR*	IL	64551	71326	71434	64552
315847	*	**XR**	E	*XR*	IL	64553	71327	71435	64554
315848	*	**XR**	E	*XR*	IL	64555	71328	71436	64556
315849	*	**XR**	E	*XR*	IL	64557	71329	71437	64558
315850	*	**XR**	E	*XR*	IL	64559	71330	71438	64560
315851	*	**XR**	E	*XR*	IL	64561	71331	71439	64562
315852	*	**XR**	E	*XR*	IL	64563	71332	71440	64564
315853	*	**XR**	E	*XR*	IL	64565	71333	71441	64566
315854	*	**XR**	E	*XR*	IL	64567	71334	71442	64568
315855	*	**XR**	E	*XR*	IL	64569	71335	71443	64570
315856	*	**XR**	E	*XR*	IL	64571	71336	71444	64572
315857	*	**XR**	E	*XR*	IL	64573	71337	71445	64574
315858	*	**XR**	E	*XR*	IL	64575	71338	71446	64576
315859	*	**XR**	E	*XR*	IL	64577	71339	71447	64578
315860	*	**XR**	E	*XR*	IL	64579	71340	71448	64580
315861	*	**XR**	E	*XR*	IL	64581	71341	71449	64582

Names (carried on DMSO):

315817	Transport for London
315829	London Borough of Havering Celebrating 40 years
315845	Herbie Woodward

CLASS 317   BREL YORK/DERBY

Outer suburban units.

Formation: Various, see sub-class headings.
Construction: Steel.
Traction Motors: Four GEC G315BZ of 247.5 kW (except 317 722, see below).
Wheel Arrangement: 2-2 + Bo-Bo + 2-2 + 2-2.
Braking: Disc.   **Dimensions:** 19.83/20.18 x 2.82 m.
Bogies: BP20 (MSO), BT13 (others).   **Couplers:** Tightlock.
Gangways: Throughout   **Control System:** Thyristor.
Doors: Sliding.   **Maximum Speed:** 100 mph.
Seating Layout: Various, see sub-class headings.
Multiple Working: Within class & with Classes 318, 319, 320, 321, 322 and 323.

Class 317/1. Pressure ventilated.

Formation: DTSO–MSO–TCO–DTSO.
Seating Layout: 1: 2+2 facing, 2: 3+2 facing.

DTSO(A) Lot No. 30955 York 1981–82. –/74. 29.5 t.
MSO. Lot No. 30958 York 1981–82. –/79. 49.0 t.
TCO. Lot No. 30957 Derby 1981–82. 22/46 2T. 29.0 t.
DTSO(B) Lot No. 30956 York 1981–82. –/71. 29.5 t.

317337	**TL**	A	*GN*	HE	77036	62671	71613	77084
317338	**TL**	A	*GN*	HE	77037	62698	71614	77085
317339	**TL**	A	*GN*	HE	77038	62699	71615	77086
317340	**TL**	A	*GN*	HE	77039	62700	71616	77087

317341	**TL**	A	*GN*	HE	77040	62701	71617	77088
317342	**TL**	A	*GN*	HE	77041	62702	71618	77089
317343	**TL**	A	*GN*	HE	77042	62703	71619	77090
317344	**FU**	A	*GN*	HE	77029	62690	71620	77091
317345	**FU**	A	*GN*	HE	77044	62705	71621	77092
317346	**FU**	A	*GN*	HE	77045	62706	71622	77093
317347	**FU**	A	*GN*	HE	77046	62707	71623	77094
317348	**FU**	A	*GN*	HE	77047	62708	71624	77095

Names (carried on TCO):

317345 Driver John Webb | 317348 Richard A Jenner

Class 317/5. Pressure ventilated. Units renumbered from Class 317/1 in 2005 for West Anglia Metro services. Refurbished with new upholstery and Passenger Information Systems. Details as Class 317/1.

The original DTSO 77048 was written off after the Cricklewood accident of 1983. A replacement vehicle was built (at Wolverton) in 1987 and given the same number.

317501	**GA**	A	*GA*	IL	77024	62661	71577	77048ǁ
317502	**GA**	A	*GA*	IL	77001	62662	71578	77049
317503	**GA**	A	*GA*	IL	77002	62663	71579	77050
317504	**GA**	A	*GA*	IL	77003	62664	71580	77051
317505	**GA**	A	*GA*	IL	77004	62665	71581	77052
317506	**GA**	A	*GA*	IL	77005	62666	71582	77053
317507	**GA**	A	*GA*	IL	77006	62667	71583	77054
317508	**GA**	A	*GA*	IL	77010	62697	71587	77058
317509	**GA**	A	*GA*	IL	77011	62672	71588	77059
317510	**GA**	A	*GA*	IL	77012	62673	71589	77060
317511	**NC**	A	*GA*	IL	77014	62675	71591	77062
317512	**NC**	A	*GA*	IL	77015	62676	71592	77063
317513	**GA**	A	*GA*	IL	77016	62677	71593	77064
317514	**GA**	A	*GA*	IL	77017	62678	71594	77065
317515	**GA**	A	*GA*	IL	77019	62680	71596	77067

Name (carried on TCO):

317507 University of Cambridge 800 Years 1209–2009

Class 317/6. Convection heating. Units converted from Class 317/2 by Railcare, Wolverton 1998–99 with Chapman seating.

Formation: DTSO–MSO–TSO–DTCO.
Seating Layout: 2+2 facing.

77200–219. DTSO. Lot No. 30994 York 1985–86. –/64. 29.5 t.
77280–283. DTSO. Lot No. 31007 York 1987. –/64. 29.5 t.
62846–865. MSO. Lot No. 30996 York 1985–86. –/71. 49.0 t.
62886–889. MSO. Lot No. 31009 York 1987. –/71. 49.0 t.
71734–753. TSO. Lot No. 30997 York 1985–86. –/60(+3) 2T. 29.0 t.
71762–765. TSO. Lot No. 31010 York 1987. –/60(+3) 2T. 29.0 t.
77220–239. DTCO. Lot No. 30995 York 1985–86. 24/36. 29.5 t.
77284–287. DTCO. Lot No. 31008 York 1987. 24/36. 29.5 t.

317649	NC	A	GA	IL	77200	62846	71734	77220
317650	NC	A	GA	IL	77201	62847	71735	77221
317651	NC	A	GA	IL	77202	62848	71736	77222
317652	NC	A	GA	IL	77203	62849	71739	77223
317653	NC	A	GA	IL	77204	62850	71738	77224
317654	NC	A	GA	IL	77205	62851	71737	77225
317655	GA	A	GA	IL	77206	62852	71740	77226
317656	NC	A	GA	IL	77207	62853	71742	77227
317657	NC	A	GA	IL	77208	62854	71741	77228
317658	GA	A	GA	IL	77209	62855	71743	77229
317659	GA	A	GA	IL	77210	62856	71744	77230
317660	GA	A	GA	IL	77211	62857	71745	77231
317661	GA	A	GA	IL	77212	62858	71746	77232
317662	GA	A	GA	IL	77213	62859	71747	77233
317663	GA	A	GA	IL	77214	62860	71748	77234
317664	GA	A	GA	IL	77215	62861	71749	77235
317665	GA	A	GA	IL	77216	62862	71750	77236
317666	NC	A	GA	IL	77217	62863	71752	77237
317667	GA	A	GA	IL	77218	62864	71751	77238
317668	GA	A	GA	IL	77219	62865	71753	77239
317669	NC	A	GA	IL	77280	62886	71762	77284
317670	GA	A	GA	IL	77281	62887	71763	77285
317671	NC	A	GA	IL	77282	62888	71764	77286
317672	GA	A	GA	IL	77283	62889	71765	77287

Name (carried on DTCO): 317654   Richard Wells

Class 317/7. Units converted from Class 317/1 by Railcare, Wolverton 2000 for Stansted Express services between London Liverpool Street and Stansted. Air conditioning. Fitted with luggage stacks. Displaced from Stansted services in 2011 by Class 379s – most taken on by London Overground from May 2015.

* 317722 has received new Bombardier MJA 280-8 AC traction motors as part of an Angel trial. Two vehicles (77021 and 62682, now in **GA** livery) have also received an interior refurbishment with new Fainsa seating whilst the other two vehicles have been left in their former Stansted Express condition (and still in **NX** livery). In use with Abellio Greater Anglia as a demonstrator.

Formation: DTSO–MSO–TSO–DTCO.
Seating Layout: 1: 2+1 facing, 2: 2+2 facing.

DTSO Lot No. 30955 York 1981–82. –/52 + catering point. 31.4 t.
MSO. Lot No. 30958 York 1981–82. –/62 (* –/64). 51.3 t.
TSO. Lot No. 30957 Derby 1981–82. –/42(+5) 1W 1T 1TD. 30.2 t.
DTCO Lot No. 30956 York 1981–82. 22/16 + catering point. 31.6 t.

317708		LO	A	LO	IL	77007	62668	71584	77055
317709		LO	A	LO	IL	77008	62669	71585	77056
317710		LO	A	LO	IL	77009	62670	71586	77057
317714		LO	A	LO	IL	77013	62674	71590	77061
317719		NX	A	LO	IL	77018	62679	71595	77066
317722	*	GA/NX	A	GA	IL	77021	62682	71598	77069
317723		GA	A	LO	IL	77022	62683	71599	77070

| 317729 | **LO** | A | *LO* | IL | 77028 | 62689 | 71605 | 77076 |
| 317732 | **GA** | A | *LO* | IL | 77031 | 62692 | 71608 | 77079 |

Class 317/8. Pressure Ventilated. Units refurbished and renumbered from Class 317/1 in 2005–06 at Wabtec, Doncaster for use on Stansted Express services. Displaced from Stansted services in 2011.

Formation: DTSO–MSO–TCO–DTSO.
Seating Layout: 1: 2+2 facing, 2: 3+2 facing.

DTSO(A) Lot No. 30955 York 1981–82. –/66. 29.5 t.
MSO. Lot No. 30958 York 1981–82. –/71. 49.0 t.
TCO. Lot No. 30957 Derby 1981–82. 20/42 2T. 29.0 t.
DTSO(B) Lot No. 30956 York 1981–82. –/66. 29.5 t.

317881	**NX**	A	*GA*	IL	77020	62681	71597	77068	
317882	**NC**	A	*GA*	IL	77023	62684	71600	77071	
317883	**NC**	A	*GA*	IL	77000	62685	71601	77072	
317884	**NC**	A	*GA*	IL	77025	62686	71602	77073	
317885	**NC**	A	*GA*	IL	77026	62687	71603	77074	
317886	**NC**	A	*GA*	IL	77027	62688	71604	77075	
317887	**NX**	A	*LO*	IL	77043	62704	71606	77077	
317888	**NX**	A	*LO*	IL	77030	62691	71607	77078	
317889	**NX**	A	*LO*	IL	77032	62693	71609	77080	
317890	**NX**	A	*LO*	IL	77033	62694	71610	77081	
317891	**NX**	A	*LO*	IL	77034	62695	71611	77082	
317892	**NX**	A	*LO*	IL	77035	62696	71612	77083	Ilford Depot

CLASS 318   BREL YORK

Outer suburban units. An refurbishment programme is underway that involves fitted a new universal access toilet to comply with the 2020 accessibility regulations (units in **SR** livery).

Formation: DTSO–MSO–DTSO.
Construction: Steel.
Traction Motors: Four Brush TM 2141 of 268 kW.
Wheel Arrangement: 2-2 + Bo-Bo + 2-2.

Braking: Disc.	**Dimensions:** 19.83/19.92 x 2.82 m.
Bogies: BP20 (MSO), BT13 (others).	**Couplers:** Tightlock.
Gangways: Within unit.	**Control System:** Thyristor.
Doors: Sliding.	**Maximum Speed:** 90 mph.

Seating Layout: 3+2 facing.
Multiple Working: Within class & with Classes 317, 319, 320, 321, 322 and 323.

77240–259. DTSO. Lot No. 30999 1985–86. –/64 1T (–/55 1TD 2W). 30.0 t (* 32.0 t).
77288. DTSO. Lot No. 31020 1987. –/64 1T. 30.0 t.
62866–885. MSO. Lot No. 30998 1985–86. –/77 (* –/79). 50.9 t (* 53.0 t).
62890. MSO. Lot No. 31019 1987. –/77. 50.9 t.
77260–279. DTSO. Lot No. 31000 1985–86. –/72 (* –/74). 29.6 t (* 31.6 t).
77289. DTSO. Lot No. 31021 1987. –/72. 29.6 t.

| 318250 | | **SC** | E | *SR* | GW | 77240 | 62866 | 77260 |
| 318251 | * | **SR** | E | *SR* | GW | 77241 | 62867 | 77261 |

318252	*	**SR**	E	*SR*	GW	77242	62868	77262
318253	*	**SR**	E	*SR*	GW	77243	62869	77263
318254	*	**SR**	E	*SR*	GW	77244	62870	77264
318255		**SC**	E	*SR*	GW	77245	62871	77265
318256		**SC**	E	*SR*	GW	77246	62872	77266
318257	*	**SR**	E	*SR*	GW	77247	62873	77267
318258	*	**SR**	E	*SR*	GW	77248	62874	77268
318259	*	**SR**	E	*SR*	GW	77249	62875	77269
318260		**SC**	E	*SR*	GW	77250	62876	77270
318261		**SC**	E	*SR*	GW	77251	62877	77271
318262	*	**SR**	E	*SR*	GW	77252	62878	77272
318263	*	**SR**	E	*SR*	GW	77253	62879	77273
318264	*	**SR**	E	*SR*	GW	77254	62880	77274
318265	*	**SR**	E	*SR*	GW	77255	62881	77275
318266	*	**SR**	E	*SR*	GW	77256	62882	77276
318267		**SC**	E	*SR*	GW	77257	62883	77277
318268		**SC**	E	*SR*	GW	77258	62884	77278
318269		**SC**	E	*SR*	GW	77259	62885	77279
318270	*	**SR**	E	*SR*	GW	77288	62890	77289

CLASS 319   BREL YORK

Express and outer suburban units. A refurbishment programme is underway
that involves fitting a new universal access toilet to comply with the 2020
accessibility regulations (units shown *).

Formation: Various, see sub-class headings.
Systems: 25 kV AC overhead/750 V DC third rail.
Construction: Steel.
Traction Motors: Four GEC G315BZ of 268 kW.
Wheel Arrangement: 2-2 + Bo-Bo + 2-2 + 2-2.
Braking: Disc.   **Dimensions:** 20.17/20.16 x 2.82 m.
Bogies: P7-4 (MSO), T3-7 (others). **Couplers:** Tightlock.
Gangways: Within unit + end doors. **Control System:** GTO chopper.
Doors: Sliding.   **Maximum Speed:** 100 mph.
Seating Layout: Various, see sub-class headings.
Multiple Working: Within class & with Classes 317, 318, 320, 321, 322 and 323.

Class 319/0. DTSO–MSO–TSO–DTSO.

Seating Layout: 3+2 facing.

DTSO(A). Lot No. 31022 (odd nos.) 1987–88. –/82 (* –/79). 28.2 t (* 30.7 t).
MSO. Lot No. 31023 1987–88. –/82 (* –/81). 49.2 t (* 50.9 t)..
TSO. Lot No. 31024 1987–88. –/77 2T (* –/63 1TD 2W). 31.0 t (* 32.5 t)..
DTSO(B). Lot No. 31025 (even nos.) 1987–88. –/78 (* –/79). 28.1 t (* 30.0 t).

319001		**TL**	P	*TL*	BF	77291	62891	71772	77290
319002	*	**TL**	P	*TL*	BF	77293	62892	71773	77292
319003	*	**TL**	P	*TL*	BF	77295	62893	71774	77294
319004		**TL**	P		ZN	77297	62894	71775	77296
319005	*	**TL**	P		ZN	77299	62895	71776	77298
319006	*	**TL**	P	*TL*	BF	77301	62896	71777	77300

319007	*	**TL**	P	*TL*	BF	77303	62897	71778	77302
319008	*	**TL**	P	*TL*	BF	77305	62898	71779	77304
319009		**TL**	P	*TL*	BF	77307	62899	71780	77306
319010		**TL**	P	*TL*	BF	77309	62900	71781	77308
319011		**TL**	P	*TL*	BF	77311	62901	71782	77310
319012	*	**TL**	P	*TL*	BF	77313	62902	71783	77312
319013		**LM**	P	*LM*	NN	77315	62903	71784	77314

Names (carried on TSO):

319001 Driver Mick Winnett	319009 Coquelles
319008 Cheriton	319011 John Ruskin College

Class 319/2. DTSO–MSO–TSO–DTCO. Units converted from Class 319/0.

Seating Layout: 1: 2+1 facing, 2: 2+2/3+2 facing.

DTSO. Lot No. 31022 (odd nos.) 1987–88. –/64. 30.0 t.
MSO. Lot No. 31023 1987–88. –/73. 51.0 t.
TSO. Lot No. 31024 1987–88. –/52 1T 1TD. 31.0 t.
DTCO. Lot No. 31025 (even nos.) 1987–88. 18/36. 30.0 t.

319214	*	**TL**	P	*TL*	BF	77317	62904	71785	77316
319215	*	**TL**	P	*TL*	BF	77319	62905	71786	77318
319216	*	**LM**	P	*LM*	NN	77321	62906	71787	77320
319217	*	**TL**	P	*TL*	BF	77323	62907	71788	77322 Brighton
319218	*	**TL**	P	*NO*	AN	77325	62908	71789	77324
319219	*	**TL**	P	*NO*	AN	77327	62909	71790	77326
319220	*	**TL**	P	*TL*	BF	77329	62910	71791	77328

Class 319/3. DTSO–MSO–TSO–DTSO. Converted from Class 319/1 by replacing First Class seats with Standard Class seats.

20 units transferred to Northern for services around Manchester and Liverpool in 2014–15.

Seating Layout: 3+2 facing.

DTSO(A). Lot No. 31063 1990. –/72. 29.0 t.
MSO. Lot No. 31064 1990. –/79. 50.6 t.
TSO. Lot No. 31065 1990. –/74 2T. 31.0 t.
DTSO(B). Lot No. 31066 1990. –/77 2W. 29.7 t.

319361		**NP**	P	*NO*	AN	77459	63043	71929	77458
319362		**NP**	P	*NO*	AN	77461	63044	71930	77460
319363		**NP**	P	*NO*	AN	77463	63045	71931	77462
319364		**NP**	P	*NO*	AN	77465	63046	71932	77464
319365		**NP**	P	*NO*	AN	77467	63047	71933	77466
319366		**NP**	P	*NO*	AN	77469	63048	71934	77468
319367		**NP**	P	*NO*	AN	77471	63049	71935	77470
319368		**NP**	P	*NO*	AN	77473	63050	71936	77472
319369		**NP**	P	*NO*	AN	77475	63051	71937	77474
319370		**FU**	P	*TL*	BF	77477	63052	71938	77476
319371		**NP**	P	*NO*	AN	77479	63053	71939	77478
319372	*	**TL**	P	*TL*	BF	77481	63054	71940	77480
319373		**TL**	P	*TL*	BF	77483	63055	71941	77482

319374	NP	P	NO	AN	77485	63056	71942	77484
319375	NP	P	NO	AN	77487	63057	71943	77486
319376	NP	P	NO	AN	77489	63058	71944	77488
319377	NP	P	NO	AN	77491	63059	71945	77490
319378	NP	P	NO	AN	77493	63060	71946	77492
319379	NP	P	NO	AN	77495	63061	71947	77494
319380	NP	P	NO	AN	77497	63062	71948	77496
319381	FU	P	TL	BF	77973	63093	71979	77974
319382	NP	P	NO	AN	77975	63094	71980	77976
319383	NP	P	NO	AN	77977	63095	71981	77978
319384	FU	P	TL	BF	77979	63096	71982	77980
319385	FU	P	TL	BF	77981	63097	71983	77982
319386	NP	P	NO	AN	77983	63098	71984	77984

Name (carried on TSO): 319362   Northern Powerhouse

Class 319/4. DTCO–MSO–TSO–DTSO. Converted from Class 319/0. Refurbished with carpets. DTSO(A) converted to composite.

Seating Layout: 1: 2+1 facing 2: 2+2/3+2 facing.

Non-standard liveries: 319 429 & 319 460 White with grey doors.

77331–381. DTCO. Lot No. 31022 (odd nos.) 1987–88. 12/51 (* 12/50). 30.0t (* 31.0 t).
77441–457. DTCO. Lot No. 31038 (odd nos.) 1988. 12/51 (* 12/50). 30.0t (* 31.0 t).
62911–936. MSO. Lot No. 31023 1987–88. –/74 (* –/75). 49.2 t (* 52.4 t).
62961–974. MSO. Lot No. 31039 1988. –/74 (* –/75). 49.2 t (* 52.4 t).
71792–817. TSO. Lot No. 31024 1987–88. –/67 2T (* –/58 1TD 2W). 31.0 t (* 33.7 t).
71866–879. TSO. Lot No. 31040 1988. –/67 2T (* –/58 1TD 2W). 31.0 t (* 33.7 t).
77330–380. DTSO. Lot No. 31025 (even nos.) 1987–88. –/71 1W (* –/73). 28.1t (* 30.7 t).
77430–456. DTSO. Lot No. 31041 (even nos.) 1988. –/71 1W (* –/73). 28.1t (* 30.7 t).

319421	*	TL	P	TL	BF	77331	62911	71792	77330
319422	*	TL	P	TL	BF	77333	62912	71793	77332
319423	*	TL	P	TL	BF	77335	62913	71794	77334
319424	*	TL	P	TL	BF	77337	62914	71795	77336
319425	*	TL	P	TL	BF	77339	62915	71796	77338
319426	*	TL	P	TL	BF	77341	62916	71797	77340
319427	*	TL	P	TL	BF	77343	62917	71798	77342
319428	*	TL	P	TL	BF	77345	62918	71799	77344
319429		0	P	LM	NN	77347	62919	71800	77346
319430	*	TL	P	TL	BF	77349	62920	71801	77348
319431	*	TL	P		ZN	77351	62921	71802	77350
319432	*	TL	P	TL	BF	77353	62922	71803	77352
319433	*	TL	P	TL	BF	77355	62923	71804	77354
319434	*	TL	P	TL	BF	77357	62924	71805	77356
319435	*	TL	P	TL	BF	77359	62925	71806	77358
319436	*	TL	P	TL	BF	77361	62926	71807	77360
319437	*	TL	P	TL	BF	77363	62927	71808	77362
319438	*	TL	P	TL	BF	77365	62928	71809	77364
319439	*	TL	P	TL	BF	77367	62929	71810	77366
319440	*	TL	P	TL	BF	77369	62930	71811	77368
319441		FU	P	LM	NN	77371	62931	71812	77370
319442		FU	P		ZN	77373	62932	71813	77372

319443	*	**TL**	P	*TL*	BF	77375	62933	71814	77374
319444	*	**TL**	P	*TL*	BF	77377	62934	71815	77376
319445	*	**TL**	P	*TL*	BF	77379	62935	71816	77378
319446	*	**TL**	P	*TL*	BF	77381	62936	71817	77380
319447	*	**TL**	P	*TL*	BF	77431	62961	71866	77430
319448		**FU**	P		ZN	77433	62962	71867	77432
319449	*	**TL**	P	*TL*	BF	77435	62963	71868	77434
319450		**FU**	P	*TL*	BF	77437	62964	71869	77436
319451		**FU**	P	*TL*	BF	77439	62965	71870	77438
319452		**FU**	P	*TL*	BF	77441	62966	71871	77440
319453		**FU**	P	*TL*	BF	77443	62967	71872	77442
319454		**FU**	P	*TL*	BF	77445	62968	71873	77444
319455		**FU**	P	*LM*	NN	77447	62969	71874	77446
319456	*	**TL**	P	*TL*	BF	77449	62970	71875	77448
319457		**FU**	P	*LM*	NN	77451	62971	71876	77450
319458	*	**TL**	P	*TL*	BF	77453	62972	71877	77452
319459	*	**TL**	P	*TL*	BF	77455	62973	71878	77454
319460		**0**	P	*LM*	NN	77457	62974	71879	77456

Name (carried on TSO): 319444 City of St Albans

CLASS 320 BREL YORK

Suburban units. All 320/3s refurbished 2011–13 and fitted with a new universal access toilet to comply with the 2020 accessibility regulations. In 2016 ScotRail is receiving 320411–417 (ex-321411–417) reformed as 3-cars.

Formation: DTSO–MSO–DTSO.
Construction: Steel
Traction Motors: Four Brush TM2141B of 268 kW.
Wheel Arrangement: 2-2 + Bo-Bo + 2-2.
Braking: Disc.   **Dimensions:** 19.95 x 2.82 m.
Bogies: P7-4 (MSO), T3-7 (others).   **Couplers:** Tightlock.
Gangways: Within unit.   **Control System:** Thyristor.
Doors: Sliding.   **Maximum Speed:** 90 mph.
Seating Layout: 3+2 facing.
Multiple Working: Within class & with Classes 317, 318, 319, 321, 322 and 323.

Class 320/3. Original build.

DTSO (A). Lot No. 31060 1990. –/51(+4) 1TD 2W. 31.7 t.
MSO. Lot No. 31062 1990. –/78. 52.6 t.
DTSO (B). Lot No. 31061 1990. –/77. 31.6 t.

320301	**SR**	E	*SR*	GW	77899	63021	77921
320302	**SR**	E	*SR*	GW	77900	63022	77922
320303	**SR**	E	*SR*	GW	77901	63023	77923
320304	**SR**	E	*SR*	GW	77902	63024	77924
320305	**SR**	E	*SR*	GW	77903	63025	77925
320306	**SR**	E	*SR*	GW	77904	63026	77926
320307	**SR**	E	*SR*	GW	77905	63027	77927
320308	**SR**	E	*SR*	GW	77906	63028	77928
320309	**SR**	E	*SR*	GW	77907	63029	77929

320310	**SR**	E	*SR*	GW	77908	63030	77930
320311	**SR**	E	*SR*	GW	77909	63031	77931
320312	**SR**	E	*SR*	GW	77910	63032	77932
320313	**SR**	E	*SR*	GW	77911	63033	77933
320314	**SR**	E	*SR*	GW	77912	63034	77934
320315	**SR**	E	*SR*	GW	77913	63035	77935
320316	**SR**	E	*SR*	GW	77914	63036	77936
320317	**SR**	E	*SR*	GW	77915	63037	77937
320318	**SR**	E	*SR*	GW	77916	63038	77938
320319	**SR**	E	*SR*	GW	77917	63039	77939
320320	**SR**	E	*SR*	GW	77918	63040	77940
320321	**SR**	E	*SR*	GW	77919	63041	77941
320322	**SR**	E	*SR*	GW	77920	63042	77942

Class 320/4. Former London Midland Class 321s reduced to 3-car formation and refurbished as Class 320/4s by Wabtec Doncaster 2015–16. Full details awaited.

DTSO (A). Lot No. 31060 1990.   .   t.
MSO. Lot No. 31062 1990.   .   t.
DTSO (B). Lot No. 31061 1990.   .   t.

320411	(321411)	**SR**	E	*SR*	GW	78105	63073	77953
320412	(321412)	**SR**	E	*SR*	GW	78106	63074	77954
320413	(321413)	**SR**	E	*SR*	GW	78107	63075	77955
320414	(321414)	**SR**	E	*SR*	GW	78108	63076	77956
320415	(321415)	**SR**	E	*SR*	GW	78109	63077	77957
320416	(321416)	**SR**	E	*SR*	GW	78110	63078	77958
320417	(321417)	**SR**	E	*SR*	GW	78111	63079	77959

CLASS 321   BREL YORK

Outer suburban units.

Formation: DTCO (DTSO on Class 321/9)–MSO–TSO–DTSO.
Construction: Steel.
Traction Motors: Four Brush TM2141C of 268 kW.
Wheel Arrangement: 2-2 + Bo-Bo + 2-2 + 2-2.
Braking: Disc.   **Dimensions:** 19.95 x 2.82 m.
Bogies: P7-4 (MSO), T3-7 (others).   **Couplers:** Tightlock.
Gangways: Within unit.   **Control System:** Thyristor.
Doors: Sliding.   **Maximum Speed:** 100 mph.
Seating Layout: 1: 2+2 facing, 2: 3+2 facing.
Multiple Working: Within class & with Classes 317, 318, 319, 320, 322 and 323.

Class 321/3.

* "Renatus" rebuilt units with completely new interiors. Full details awaited.

DTCO. Lot No. 31053 1988–90. 16/57 (321 347–366 16/56). 29.7 t.
MSO. Lot No. 31054 1988–90. –/82. 51.5 t.
TSO. Lot No. 31055 1988–90. –/75 2T. 29.1 t.
DTSO. Lot No. 31056 1988–90. –/78. 29.7 t.

321 301		**NX**	E	*GA*	IL	78049	62975	71880	77853
321 302		**NX**	E	*GA*	IL	78050	62976	71881	77854
321 303	*	**GA**	E	*GA*	IL	78051	62977	71882	77855
321 304	*	**NX**	E	*GA*	IL	78052	62978	71883	77856
321 305		**NX**	E	*GA*	IL	78053	62979	71884	77857
321 306		**NX**	E	*GA*	IL	78054	62980	71885	77858
321 307		**NX**	E	*GA*	IL	78055	62981	71886	77859
321 308		**NX**	E	*GA*	IL	78056	62982	71887	77860
321 309		**NX**	E	*GA*	IL	78057	62983	71888	77861
321 310		**NX**	E	*GA*	IL	78058	62984	71889	77862
321 311		**NX**	E	*GA*	IL	78059	62985	71890	77863
321 312		**NX**	E	*GA*	IL	78060	62986	71891	77864
321 313		**NX**	E	*GA*	IL	78061	62987	71892	77865
321 314		**NX**	E	*GA*	IL	78062	62988	71893	77866
321 315		**NX**	E	*GA*	IL	78063	62989	71894	77867
321 316		**NX**	E	*GA*	IL	78064	62990	71895	77868
321 317		**NX**	E	*GA*	IL	78065	62991	71896	77869
321 318		**NX**	E	*GA*	IL	78066	62992	71897	77870
321 319		**NX**	E	*GA*	IL	78067	62993	71898	77871
321 320		**NX**	E	*GA*	IL	78068	62994	71899	77872
321 321	*	**NX**	E	*GA*	IL	78069	62995	71900	77873
321 322		**NX**	E	*GA*	IL	78070	62996	71901	77874
321 323		**NX**	E	*GA*	IL	78071	62997	71902	77875
321 324		**NX**	E	*GA*	IL	78072	62998	71903	77876
321 325		**NX**	E	*GA*	IL	78073	62999	71904	77877
321 326		**NX**	E	*GA*	IL	78074	63000	71905	77878
321 327		**NC**	E	*GA*	IL	78075	63001	71906	77879
321 328		**NX**	E	*GA*	IL	78076	63002	71907	77880
321 329		**NX**	E	*GA*	IL	78077	63003	71908	77881
321 330		**NC**	E	*GA*	IL	78078	63004	71909	77882
321 331		**NC**	E	*GA*	IL	78079	63005	71910	77883
321 332		**NC**	E	*GA*	IL	78080	63006	71911	77884
321 333		**NC**	E	*GA*	IL	78081	63007	71912	77885
321 334		**NC**	E	*GA*	IL	78082	63008	71913	77886
321 335		**NC**	E	*GA*	IL	78083	63009	71914	77887
321 336		**NC**	E	*GA*	IL	78084	63010	71915	77888
321 337		**NC**	E	*GA*	IL	78085	63011	71916	77889
321 338		**NC**	E	*GA*	IL	78086	63012	71917	77890
321 339		**NC**	E	*GA*	IL	78087	63013	71918	77891
321 340		**NC**	E	*GA*	IL	78088	63014	71919	77892
321 341		**NC**	E	*GA*	IL	78089	63015	71920	77893
321 342		**NC**	E	*GA*	IL	78090	63016	71921	77894
321 343		**NC**	E	*GA*	IL	78091	63017	71922	77895
321 344		**NC**	E	*GA*	IL	78092	63018	71923	77896
321 345		**NC**	E	*GA*	IL	78093	63019	71924	77897
321 346		**NC**	E	*GA*	IL	78094	63020	71925	77898
321 347		**NC**	E	*GA*	IL	78131	63105	71991	78280
321 348		**NC**	E	*GA*	IL	78132	63106	71992	78281
321 349		**NC**	E	*GA*	IL	78133	63107	71993	78282
321 350		**NC**	E	*GA*	IL	78134	63108	71994	78283
321 351		**NC**	E	*GA*	IL	78135	63109	71995	78284

321 352	**NC**	E	*GA*	IL	78136	63110	71996	78285
321 353	**NC**	E	*GA*	IL	78137	63111	71997	78286
321 354	**NC**	E	*GA*	IL	78138	63112	71998	78287
321 355	**NC**	E	*GA*	IL	78139	63113	71999	78288
321 356	**NC**	E	*GA*	IL	78140	63114	72000	78289
321 357	**NC**	E	*GA*	IL	78141	63115	72001	78290
321 358	**NC**	E	*GA*	IL	78142	63116	72002	78291
321 359	**GA**	E	*GA*	IL	78143	63117	72003	78292
321 360	**NC**	E	*GA*	IL	78144	63118	72004	78293
321 361	**GA**	E	*GA*	IL	78145	63119	72005	78294
321 362	**GA**	E	*GA*	IL	78146	63120	72006	78295
321 363	**GA**	E	*GA*	IL	78147	63121	72007	78296
321 364	**GA**	E	*GA*	IL	78148	63122	72008	78297
321 365	**GA**	E	*GA*	IL	78149	63123	72009	78298
321 366	**GA**	E	*GA*	IL	78150	63124	72010	78299

Names (carried on TSO):

321 312	Southend-on-Sea
321 313	University of Essex
321 321	NSPCC ESSEX FULL STOP
321 334	Amsterdam
321 336	GEOFFREY FREEMAN ALLEN
321 342	R. Barnes
321 343	RSA RAILWAY STUDY ASSOCIATION
321 351	London Southend Airport
321 361	Phoenix

Class 321/4.

The original vehicles 71966 and 77960 from 321418 and 78114 and 63082 from 321420 were written off after the Watford Junction accident in 1996. The undamaged vehicles were formed together as 321418 whilst four new vehicles were built in 1997, taking the same numbers as the scrapped vehicles, and these became the second 321420.

The DTCOs of 321421–437 have had 12 First Class seats declassified.

Units 321 411–417 have been refurbished as Class 320/4 3-car units for ScotRail (their TSO vehicles are stored).

† 321448 has received an interior refurbishment as an Eversholt demonstrator unit. It has been fitted with two different types of interior using seats supplied by ATD. 78130 and 63104 have a "suburban" interior with a 3+2 seating layout and 78279 and 71990 have a "metro" interior with 2+2 seating. It is also being used as a testbed unit for the fitting of new AC traction equipment.

Non-standard livery: 321448 Eversholt demonstrator (silver with blue doors and multi-coloured stripes).

DTCO. Lot No. 31067 1989–90. 28/40 (321 421–437 16/52, 321 438–447 16/56). 29.8 t. († 16/30(+4) 1TD 2W 33.9 t).
MSO. Lot No. 31068 1989–90. –/79 (321 438–447 –/82). 51.6 t († –/82. 54.0 t).
TSO. Lot No. 31069 1989–90. –/74 2T (321 438–447 –/75 2T). 29.2 t († –/62 1T. 31.7 t).

DTSO. Lot No. 31070 1989–90. –/78. 29.8 t. († –/58. 33.2 t.).

321 401	**FU**	E	*GN*	HE	78095	63063	71949	77943
321 402	**FU**	E	*GN*	HE	78096	63064	71950	77944
321 403	**FU**	E	*GN*	HE	78097	63065	71951	77945
321 404	**FU**	E	*GN*	HE	78098	63066	71952	77946
321 405	**FU**	E	*GN*	HE	78099	63067	71953	77947
321 406	**FU**	E	*GN*	HE	78100	63068	71954	77948
321 407	**FU**	E	*GN*	HE	78101	63069	71955	77949
321 408	**FU**	E	*GN*	HE	78102	63070	71956	77950
321 409	**FU**	E	*GN*	HE	78103	63071	71957	77951
321 410	**FU**	E	*GN*	HE	78104	63072	71958	77952
321 418	**FU**	E	*GN*	HE	78112	63080	71968	77962
321 419	**FU**	E	*GN*	HE	78113	63081	71967	77961
321 420	**FU**	E	*GN*	HE	78114[II]	63082[II]	71966[II]	77960[II]
321 421	**NC**	E	*GA*	IL	78115	63083	71969	77963
321 422	**NC**	E	*GA*	IL	78116	63084	71970	77964
321 423	**NC**	E	*GA*	IL	78117	63085	71971	77965
321 424	**NX**	E	*GA*	IL	78118	63086	71972	77966
321 425	**NC**	E	*GA*	IL	78119	63087	71973	77967
321 426	**NX**	E	*GA*	IL	78120	63088	71974	77968
321 427	**NX**	E	*GA*	IL	78121	63089	71975	77969
321 428	**NX**	E	*GA*	IL	78122	63090	71976	77970
321 429	**NX**	E	*GA*	IL	78123	63091	71977	77971
321 430	**NX**	E	*GA*	IL	78124	63092	71978	77972
321 431	**NX**	E	*GA*	IL	78151	63125	72011	78300
321 432	**NC**	E	*GA*	IL	78152	63126	72012	78301
321 433	**NC**	E	*GA*	IL	78153	63127	72013	78302
321 434	**NC**	E	*GA*	IL	78154	63128	72014	78303
321 435	**NC**	E	*GA*	IL	78155	63129	72015	78304
321 436	**NC**	E	*GA*	IL	78156	63130	72016	78305
321 437	**NC**	E	*GA*	IL	78157	63131	72017	78306
321 438	**GA**	E	*GA*	IL	78158	63132	72018	78307
321 439	**GA**	E	*GA*	IL	78159	63133	72019	78308
321 440	**GA**	E	*GA*	IL	78160	63134	72020	78309
321 441	**GA**	E	*GA*	IL	78161	63135	72021	78310
321 442	**GA**	E	*GA*	IL	78162	63136	72022	78311
321 443	**GA**	E	*GA*	IL	78125	63099	71985	78274
321 444	**NC**	E	*GA*	IL	78126	63100	71986	78275
321 445	**NC**	E	*GA*	IL	78127	63101	71987	78276
321 446	**NC**	E	*GA*	IL	78128	63102	71988	78277
321 447	**GA**	E	*GA*	IL	78129	63103	71989	78278
321 448	† **0**	E	*GA*	IL	78130	63104	71990	78279
Spare	**LM**	E		ZB (S)	71959	71960	71963	71964
					71965			
Spare	**L0**	E		ZB (S)	71961	71962		

Names (carried on TSO):

321 403   Stewart Fleming Signalman King's Cross
321 409   Dame Alice Owen's School 400 Years of Learning
321 428   The Essex Commuter

321 442 Crouch Valley 1889–2014
321 444 Essex Lifeboats
321 446 George Mullings

Class 321/9. DTSO(A)–MSO–TSO–DTSO(B).

Refurbished 2015 with a new universal access toilet to comply with the 2020 accessibility regulations.

DTSO(A). Lot No. 31108 1991. –/45(+6) 1TD 2W. 31.7 t.
MSO. Lot No. 31109 1991. –/79. 52.1 t.
TSO. Lot No. 31110 1991. –/78. 30.6 t.
DTSO(B). Lot No. 31111 1991. –/79. 30.6 t.

321 901	**NB**	E	*NO*	NL	77990	63153	72128	77993
321 902	**NB**	E	*NO*	NL	77991	63154	72129	77994
321 903	**NB**	E	*NO*	NL	77992	63155	72130	77995

CLASS 322   BREL YORK

Units built for use on Stansted Airport services, used for a number of years with ScotRail before transfer to Northern. Refurbished 2014–15 with a universal access toilet to comply with the 2020 accessibility regulations.

Formation: DTSO–MSO–TSO–DTSO.
Construction: Steel.
Traction Motors: Four Brush TM2141C of 268 kW.
Wheel Arrangement: 2-2 + Bo-Bo + 2-2 + 2-2.

Braking: Disc.	**Dimensions:** 19.95/19.92 x 2.82 m.
Bogies: P7-4 (MSO), T3-7 (others).	**Couplers:** Tightlock.
Gangways: Within unit.	**Control System:** Thyristor.
Doors: Sliding.	**Maximum Speed:** 100 mph.

Seating Layout: 3+2 facing.
Multiple Working: Within class & with Classes 317, 318, 319, 320, 321 and 323.

DTSO(A). Lot No. 31094 1990. –/54(+4) 1TD 2W. 31.7 t.
MSO. Lot No. 31092 1990. –/83. 52.1 t.
TSO. Lot No. 31093 1990. –/80 1T. 30.6 t.
DTSO(B). Lot No. 31091 1990. –/79. 30.6 t.

322 481	**NB**	E	*NO*	NL	78163	63137	72023	77985
322 482	**NB**	E	*NO*	NL	78164	63138	72024	77986
322 483	**NB**	E	*NO*	NL	78165	63139	72025	77987
322 484	**NB**	E	*NO*	NL	78166	63140	72026	77988
322 485	**NB**	E	*NO*	NL	78167	63141	72027	77989

CLASS 323 HUNSLET TRANSPORTATION PROJECTS

Suburban units.

Formation: DMSO–PTSO–DMSO.
Construction: Welded aluminium alloy.
Traction Motors: Four Holec DMKT 52/24 asynchronous of 146 kW.
Wheel Arrangement: Bo-Bo + 2-2 + Bo-Bo.
Braking: Disc.   **Dimensions:** 23.37/23.44 x 2.80 m.
Bogies: SRP BP62 (DMSO), BT52 (PTSO). **Couplers:** Tightlock.
Gangways: Within unit.   **Control System:** GTO Inverter.
Doors: Sliding plug.   **Maximum Speed:** 90 mph.
Seating Layout: 3+2 facing/unidirectional.
Multiple Working: Within class & with Classes 317, 318, 319, 320, 321 and 322.

DMSO(A). Lot No. 31112 Hunslet 1992–93. –/98 († –/82). 41.0 t.
TSO. Lot No. 31113 Hunslet 1992–93. –/88(+5) 1T 2W. († –/80 1T 2W). 39.4t.
DMSO(B). Lot No. 31114 Hunslet 1992–93. –/98 († –/82). 41.0 t.

323201		**LM**	P	*LM*	SO	64001	72201	65001
323202		**LM**	P	*LM*	SO	64002	72202	65002
323203		**LM**	P	*LM*	SO	64003	72203	65003
323204		**LM**	P	*LM*	SO	64004	72204	65004
323205		**LM**	P	*LM*	SO	64005	72205	65005
323206		**LM**	P	*LM*	SO	64006	72206	65006
323207		**LM**	P	*LM*	SO	64007	72207	65007
323208		**LM**	P	*LM*	SO	64008	72208	65008
323209		**LM**	P	*LM*	SO	64009	72209	65009
323210		**LM**	P	*LM*	SO	64010	72210	65010
323211		**LM**	P	*LM*	SO	64011	72211	65011
323212		**LM**	P	*LM*	SO	64012	72212	65012
323213		**LM**	P	*LM*	SO	64013	72213	65013
323214		**LM**	P	*LM*	SO	64014	72214	65014
323215		**LM**	P	*LM*	SO	64015	72215	65015
323216		**LM**	P	*LM*	SO	64016	72216	65016
323217		**LM**	P	*LM*	SO	64017	72217	65017
323218		**LM**	P	*LM*	SO	64018	72218	65018
323219		**LM**	P	*LM*	SO	64019	72219	65019
323220		**LM**	P	*LM*	SO	64020	72220	65020
323221		**LM**	P	*LM*	SO	64021	72221	65021
323222		**LM**	P	*LM*	SO	64022	72222	65022
323223	†	**NO**	P	*NO*	LG	64023	72223	65023
323224	†	**NO**	P	*NO*	LG	64024	72224	65024
323225	†	**NO**	P	*NO*	LG	64025	72225	65025
323226		**NO**	P	*NO*	LG	64026	72226	65026
323227		**NO**	P	*NO*	LG	64027	72227	65027
323228		**NO**	P	*NO*	LG	64028	72228	65028
323229		**NO**	P	*NO*	LG	64029	72229	65029
323230		**NO**	P	*NO*	LG	64030	72230	65030
323231		**NO**	P	*NO*	LG	64031	72231	65031
323232		**NO**	P	*NO*	LG	64032	72232	65032
323233		**NO**	P	*NO*	LG	64033	72233	65033

323234	NO	P	NO	LG	64034	72234	65034
323235	NO	P	NO	LG	64035	72235	65035
323236	NO	P	NO	LG	64036	72236	65036
323237	NO	P	NO	LG	64037	72237	65037
323238	NO	P	NO	LG	64038	72238	65038
323239	NO	P	NO	LG	64039	72239	65039
323240	LM	P	LM	SO	64040	72340	65040
323241	LM	P	LM	SO	64041	72341	65041
323242	LM	P	LM	SO	64042	72342	65042
323243	LM	P	LM	SO	64043	72343	65043

CLASS 325   ABB DERBY

Postal units based on Class 319s. Compatible with diesel or electric locomotive haulage. Built for dual voltage use, but 750 V DC third rail equipment has been removed as it is not required on current duties.

Formation: DTPMV–MPMV–TPMV–DTPMV.
System: 25 kV AC overhead.
Construction: Steel.
Traction Motors: Four GEC G315BZ of 268 kW.
Wheel Arrangement: 2-2 + Bo-Bo + 2-2 + 2-2.
Braking: Disc.   **Dimensions:** 19.33 x 2.82 m.
Bogies: P7-4 (MSO), T3-7 (others).   **Couplers:** Drop-head buckeye.
Gangways: None.   **Control System:** GTO Chopper.
Doors: Roller shutter.   **Maximum Speed:** 100 mph.
Multiple Working: Within class.

DTPMV. Lot No. 31144 1995. 29.1 t.
MPMV. Lot No. 31145 1995. 49.5 t.
TPMV. Lot No. 31146 1995. 30.7 t.

325001	RL	RM	DB	CE	68300	68340	68360	68301
325002	RL	RM	DB	CE	68302	68341	68361	68303
325003	RL	RM	DB	CE	68304	68342	68362	68305
325004	RL	RM	DB	CE	68306	68343	68363	68307
325005	RM	RM	DB	CE	68308	68344	68364	68309
325006	RM	RM	DB	CE	68310	68345	68365	68311
325007	RM	RM	DB	CE	68312	68346	68366	68313
325008	RM	RM	DB	CE	68314	68347	68367	68315
325009	RL	RM	DB	CE	68316	68349	68368	68317
325011	RL	RM	DB	CE	68320	68350	68370	68321
325012	RM	RM	DB	CE	68322	68351	68371	68323
325013	RL	RM	DB	CE	68324	68352	68372	68325
325014	RL	RM	DB	CE	68326	68353	68373	68327
325015	RL	RM	DB	CE	68328	68354	68374	68329
325016	RM	RM	DB	CE	68330	68355	68375	68331

Names (carried on one side of each DTPMV):

325002 Royal Mail North Wales & North West
325006 John Grierson
325008 Peter Howarth CBE

CLASS 332   HEATHROW EXPRESS CAF/SIEMENS

Dedicated Heathrow Express units. Five units were increased from 4-car to 5-car in 2002. Usually operate in coupled pairs.

Formations: DMSO–TSO–PTSO–(TSO)–DMFO.
Construction: Steel.
Traction Motors: Two Siemens monomotors asynchronous of 350 kW.
Wheel Arrangement: B-B + 2-2 + 2-2 (+ 2-2) + B-B.
Braking: Disc.   **Dimensions:** 23.74/23.35/23.14 x 2.75 m.
Bogies: CAF.   **Couplers:** Scharfenberg 10L.
Gangways: Within unit.   **Control System:** IGBT Inverter.
Doors: Sliding plug.   **Maximum Speed:** 100 mph.
Heating & ventilation: Air conditioning.
Seating: 1: 1+1 facing/unidirectional, 2: 2+2 mainly unidirectional.
Multiple Working: Within class.

Advertising livery: Tata Communications (blue).

DMSO. CAF 1997–98. –/43(+8). 49.9 t.
72400–413. TSO. CAF 1997–98. –/64(+11). 38.4 t.
72414–418. TSO. CAF 2002. –/56 35.8 t.
PTSO. CAF 1997–98. –/39(+11) 1TD 2W. 47.6 t.
DMFO. CAF 1997–98. 20/–. 49.5 t.

332 001	**AL**	HE	*HE*	OH	78400 72412 63400		78401
332 002	**AL**	HE	*HE*	OH	78402 72409 63406		78403
332 003	**AL**	HE	*HE*	OH	78404 72407 63402		78405
332 004	**AL**	HE	*HE*	OH	78406 72405 63403		78407
332 005	**AL**	HE	*HE*	OH	78408 72411 63404	72417	78409
332 006	**AL**	HE	*HE*	OH	78410 72410 63405	72415	78411
332 007	**AL**	HE	*HE*	OH	78412 72401 63401	72414	78413
332 008	**AL**	HE	*HE*	OH	78414 72413 63407	72418	78415
332 009	**AL**	HE	*HE*	OH	78416 72400 63408	72416	78417
332 010	**AL**	HE	*HE*	OH	78418 72402 63409		78419
332 011	**AL**	HE	*HE*	OH	78420 72403 63410		78421
332 012	**AL**	HE	*HE*	OH	78422 72404 63411		78423
332 013	**AL**	HE	*HE*	OH	78424 72408 63412		78425
332 014	**AL**	HE	*HE*	OH	78426 72406 63413		78427

CLASS 333

CAF/SIEMENS

West Yorkshire area suburban units.

Formation: DMSO–PTSO–TSO–DMSO.
Construction: Steel.
Traction Motors: Two Siemens monomotors asynchronous of 350 kW.
Wheel Arrangement: B-B + 2-2 + 2-2 + B-B.
Braking: Disc.
Dimensions: 23.74 (outer ends)/23.35 (TSO) x 2.75 m.
Bogies: CAF. **Couplers:** Dellner 10L.
Gangways: Within unit. **Control System:** IGBT Inverter.
Doors: Sliding plug. **Maximum Speed:** 100 mph.
Heating & ventilation: Air conditioning.**Multiple Working:** Within class.
Seating Layout: 3+2 facing/unidirectional.

333001–008 were made up to 4-car units from 3-car units in 2002.

333009–016 were made up to 4-car units from 3-car units in 2003.

DMSO(A). (Odd Nos.) CAF 2001. –/90. 50.0 t.
PTSO. CAF 2001. –/73(+7) 1TD 2W. 46.0 t.
TSO. CAF 2002–03. –/100. 38.5 t.
DMSO(B). (Even Nos.) CAF 2001. –/90. 50.0 t.

333001	**YR**	A	*NO*	NL	78451	74461	74477	78452
333002	**YR**	A	*NO*	NL	78453	74462	74478	78454
333003	**YR**	A	*NO*	NL	78455	74463	74479	78456
333004	**YR**	A	*NO*	NL	78457	74464	74480	78458
333005	**YR**	A	*NO*	NL	78459	74465	74481	78460
333006	**YR**	A	*NO*	NL	78461	74466	74482	78462
333007	**YR**	A	*NO*	NL	78463	74467	74483	78464
333008	**YR**	A	*NO*	NL	78465	74468	74484	78466
333009	**YR**	A	*NO*	NL	78467	74469	74485	78468
333010	**YR**	A	*NO*	NL	78469	74470	74486	78470
333011	**YR**	A	*NO*	NL	78471	74471	74487	78472
333012	**YR**	A	*NO*	NL	78473	74472	74488	78474
333013	**YR**	A	*NO*	NL	78475	74473	74489	78476
333014	**YR**	A	*NO*	NL	78477	74474	74490	78478
333015	**YR**	A	*NO*	NL	78479	74475	74491	78480
333016	**YR**	A	*NO*	NL	78481	74476	74492	78482

Names (carried on end cars):

333007 Alderman J Arthur Godwin First Lord Mayor of Bradford 1907
333011 Olicana Ilkley's Roman Fort

CLASS 334 JUNIPER ALSTOM BIRMINGHAM

Outer suburban units.

Formation: DMSO–PTSO–DMSO.
Construction: Steel.
Traction Motors: Two Alstom ONIX 800 asynchronous of 270 kW.
Wheel Arrangement: 2-Bo + 2-2 + Bo-2.

Braking: Disc.
Bogies: Alstom LTB3/TBP3.
Gangways: Within unit.
Doors: Sliding plug.
Dimensions: 21.01/19.94 x 2.80 m.
Couplers: Tightlock.
Control System: IGBT Inverter.
Maximum Speed: 90 mph.
Heating & ventilation: Pressure heating and ventilation.
Seating Layout: 2+2 facing/unidirectional (3+2 in PTSO).
Multiple Working: Within class.

DMSO(A). Alstom Birmingham 1999–2001. –/64. 42.6 t.
PTSO. Alstom Birmingham 1999–2001. –/55 1TD 1W. 39.4 t.
DMSO(B). Alstom Birmingham 1999–2001. –/64. 42.6 t.

334 001	**SR**	E	*SR*	GW	64101	74301	65101
334 002	**SR**	E	*SR*	GW	64102	74302	65102
334 003	**SR**	E	*SR*	GW	64103	74303	65103
334 004	**SR**	E	*SR*	GW	64104	74304	65104
334 005	**SR**	E	*SR*	GW	64105	74305	65105
334 006	**SR**	E	*SR*	GW	64106	74306	65106
334 007	**SR**	E	*SR*	GW	64107	74307	65107
334 008	**SR**	E	*SR*	GW	64108	74308	65108
334 009	**SR**	E	*SR*	GW	64109	74309	65109
334 010	**SR**	E	*SR*	GW	64110	74310	65110
334 011	**SR**	E	*SR*	GW	64111	74311	65111
334 012	**SR**	E	*SR*	GW	64112	74312	65112
334 013	**SR**	E	*SR*	GW	64113	74313	65113
334 014	**SR**	E	*SR*	GW	64114	74314	65114
334 015	**SR**	E	*SR*	GW	64115	74315	65115
334 016	**SR**	E	*SR*	GW	64116	74316	65116
334 017	**SR**	E	*SR*	GW	64117	74317	65117
334 018	**SR**	E	*SR*	GW	64118	74318	65118
334 019	**SR**	E	*SR*	GW	64119	74319	65119
334 020	**SR**	E	*SR*	GW	64120	74320	65120
334 021	**SR**	E	*SR*	GW	64121	74321	65121
334 022	**SR**	E	*SR*	GW	64122	74322	65122
334 023	**SR**	E	*SR*	GW	64123	74323	65123
334 024	**SR**	E	*SR*	GW	64124	74324	65124
334 025	**SR**	E	*SR*	GW	64125	74325	65125
334 026	**SR**	E	*SR*	GW	64126	74326	65126
334 027	**SR**	E	*SR*	GW	64127	74327	65127
334 028	**SR**	E	*SR*	GW	64128	74328	65128
334 029	**SR**	E	*SR*	GW	64129	74329	65129
334 030	**SR**	E	*SR*	GW	64130	74330	65130
334 031	**SR**	E	*SR*	GW	64131	74331	65131
334 032	**SR**	E	*SR*	GW	64132	74332	65132
334 033	**SR**	E	*SR*	GW	64133	74333	65133
334 034	**SR**	E	*SR*	GW	64134	74334	65134
334 035	**SR**	E	*SR*	GW	64135	74335	65135
334 036	**SR**	E	*SR*	GW	64136	74336	65136
334 037	**SR**	E	*SR*	GW	64137	74337	65137
334 038	**SR**	E	*SR*	GW	64138	74338	65138
334 039	**SR**	E	*SR*	GW	64139	74339	65139
334 040	**SR**	E	*SR*	GW	64140	74340	65140

CLASS 345   AVENTRA   BOMBARDIER DERBY

9-car units currently under construction for London's Crossrail. The first 15 units will enter traffic in spring 2017 (initially as 7-car units) on Liverpool Street–Shenfield services, and then on the cross-London new Crossrail services from December 2018. The design is marketed as "Aventra" by Bombardier and is a development on the successful Electrostar design. There is an option for a further 17 9-car units. Full details awaited.

Formations: DMSO–PMSO–MSO–MSO*–TSO–MSO*–MSO–PMSO–DMSO.
* Initially these MSO vehicles will be missing from units 345 001–015.
Systems: 25 kV AC overhead.
Construction: Aluminium.
Traction Motors: Two Bombardier asynchronous of 250 kW.
Wheel Arrangement: 2-Bo + Bo-2 + Bo-Bo (+ Bo-2) + 2-2 (+ 2-Bo) + Bo-Bo + 2-Bo + Bo-2.
Braking: Disc & regenerative.
Bogies: Inside-frame.
Gangways: Within unit.
Doors: Sliding plug.
Heating & ventilation: Air conditioning.
Seating Layout: Longitudinal/2+2 facing.
Multiple Working: Within class.

Dimensions:
Couplers: Dellner.
Control System:
Maximum Speed: 90 mph.

DMSO(A). Bombardier Derby 2015–18.
PMSO(A). Bombardier Derby 2015–18.
MSO(A). Bombardier Derby 2015–18.
MSO(B). Bombardier Derby 2015–18.
TSO. Bombardier Derby 2015–18.
MSO(C). Bombardier Derby 2015–18.
MSO(D). Bombardier Derby 2015–18.
PMSO(B). Bombardier Derby 2015–18.
DMSO(B). Bombardier Derby 2015–18.

345 001	340101	340201	340301	*340401*	340501
	340601	340701	340801	340901	
345 002	340102	340202	340302	*340402*	340502
	340602	340702	340802	340902	
345 003	340103	340203	340303	*340403*	340503
	340603	340703	340803	340903	
345 004	340104	340204	340304	*340404*	340504
	340604	340704	340804	340904	
345 005	340105	340205	340305	*340405*	340505
	340605	340705	340805	340905	
345 006	340106	340206	340306	*340406*	340506
	340606	340706	340806	340906	
345 007	340107	340207	340307	*340407*	340507
	340607	340707	340807	340907	
345 008	340108	340208	340308	*340408*	340508
	340608	340708	340808	340908	
345 009	340109	340209	340309	*340409*	340509
	340609	340709	340809	340909	

345 010	340110	340210	340310	*340410*	340510
	340610	340710	340810	340910	
345 011	340111	340211	340311	*340411*	340511
	340611	340711	340811	340911	
345 012	340112	340212	340312	*340412*	340512
	340612	340712	340812	340912	
345 013	340113	340213	340313	*340413*	340513
	340613	340713	340813	340913	
345 014	340114	340214	340314	*340414*	340514
	340614	340714	340814	340914	
345 015	340115	340215	340315	*340415*	340515
	340615	340715	340815	340915	
345 016	340116	340216	340316	340416	340516
	340616	340716	340816	340916	
345 017	340117	340217	340317	340417	340517
	340617	340717	340817	340917	
345 018	340118	340218	340318	340418	340518
	340618	340718	340818	340918	
345 019	340119	340219	340319	340419	340519
	340619	340719	340819	340919	
345 020	340120	340220	340320	340420	340520
	340620	340720	340820	340920	
345 021	340121	340221	340321	340421	340521
	340621	340721	340821	340921	
345 022	340122	340222	340322	340422	340522
	340622	340722	340822	340922	
345 023	340123	340223	340323	340423	340523
	340623	340723	340823	340923	
345 024	340124	340224	340324	340424	340524
	340624	340724	340824	340924	
345 025	340125	340225	340325	340425	340525
	340625	340725	340825	340925	
345 026	340126	340226	340326	340426	340526
	340626	340726	340826	340926	
345 027	340127	340227	340327	340427	340527
	340627	340727	340827	340927	
345 028	340128	340228	340328	340428	340528
	340628	340728	340828	340928	
345 029	340129	340229	340329	340429	340529
	340629	340729	340829	340929	
345 030	340130	340230	340330	340430	340530
	340630	340730	340830	340930	
345 031	340131	340231	340331	340431	340531
	340631	340731	340831	340931	
345 032	340132	340232	340332	340432	340532
	340632	340732	340832	340932	
345 033	340133	340233	340333	340433	340533
	340633	340733	340833	340933	
345 034	340134	340234	340334	340434	340534
	340634	340734	340834	340934	

345 035	340135	340235	340335	340435	340535
	340635	340735	340835	340935	
345 036	340136	340236	340336	340436	340536
	340636	340736	340836	340936	
345 037	340137	340237	340337	340437	340537
	340637	340737	340837	340937	
345 038	340138	340238	340338	340438	340538
	340638	340738	340838	340938	
345 039	340139	340239	340339	340439	340539
	340639	340739	340839	340939	
345 040	340140	340240	340340	340440	340540
	340640	340740	340840	340940	
345 041	340141	340241	340341	340441	340541
	340641	340741	340841	340941	
345 042	340142	340242	340342	340442	340542
	340642	340742	340842	340942	
345 043	340143	340243	340343	340443	340543
	340643	340743	340843	340943	
345 044	340144	340244	340344	340444	340544
	340644	340744	340844	340944	
345 045	340145	340245	340345	340445	340545
	340645	340745	340845	340945	
345 046	340146	340246	340346	340446	340546
	340646	340746	340846	340946	
345 047	340147	340247	340347	340447	340547
	340647	340747	340847	340947	
345 048	340148	340248	340348	340448	340548
	340648	340748	340848	340948	
345 049	340149	340249	340349	340449	340549
	340649	340749	340849	340949	
345 050	340150	340250	340350	340450	340550
	340650	340750	340850	340950	
345 051	340151	340251	340351	340451	340551
	340651	340751	340851	340951	
345 052	340152	340252	340352	340452	340552
	340652	340752	340852	340952	
345 053	340153	340253	340353	340453	340553
	340653	340753	340853	340953	
345 054	340154	340254	340354	340454	340554
	340654	340754	340854	340954	
345 055	340155	340255	340355	340455	340555
	340655	340755	340855	340955	
345 056	340156	340256	340356	340456	340556
	340656	340756	340856	340956	
345 057	340157	340257	340357	340457	340557
	340657	340757	340857	340957	
345 058	340158	340258	340358	340458	340558
	340658	340758	340858	340958	
345 059	340159	340259	340359	340459	340559
	340659	340759	340859	340959	

345060	340160	340260	340360	340460	340560
	340660	340760	340860	340960	
345061	340161	340261	340361	340461	340561
	340661	340761	340861	340961	
345062	340162	340262	340362	340462	340562
	340662	340762	340862	340962	
345063	340163	340263	340363	340463	340563
	340663	340763	340863	340963	
345064	340164	340264	340364	340464	340564
	340664	340764	340864	340964	
345065	340165	340265	340365	340465	340565
	340665	340765	340865	340965	
345066	340166	340266	340366	340466	340566
	340666	340766	340866	340966	

CLASS 350   DESIRO UK   SIEMENS

Outer suburban and long distance units.

Formation: DMCO–TCO–PTSO–DMCO.
Systems: 25 kV AC overhead (350/1s built with 750 V DC).
Construction: Welded aluminium.
Traction Motors: 4 Siemens 1TB2016-0GB02 asynchronous of 250 kW.
Wheel Arrangement: Bo-Bo + 2-2 + 2-2 + Bo-Bo.
Braking: Disc & regenerative.   **Dimensions:** 20.34 x 2.79 m.
Bogies: SGP SF5000.   **Couplers:** Dellner 12.
Gangways: Throughout.   **Control System:** IGBT Inverter.
Doors: Sliding plug.
Maximum Speed: 110 mph (350/1, 350/3 & 350/4) or 100 mph (350/2).
Heating & ventilation: Air conditioning.
Seating Layout: Various, see sub-class headings.
Multiple Working: Within class.

Class 350/1. Original-build units owned by Angel Trains. Formerly part of an aborted South West Trains 5-car Class 450/2 order. 2+2 seating.

Seating Layout: 1: 2+2 facing, 2: 2+2 facing/unidirectional.

Advertising livery: 350 110 Project 110 (silver centre cars).

DMSO(A). Siemens Krefeld 2004–05. –/60. 48.7 t.
TCO. Siemens Krefeld/Prague 2004–05. 24/32 1T. 36.2 t.
PTSO. Siemens Krefeld/Prague 2004–05. –/50(+9) 1TD 2W. 45.2 t.
DMSO(B). Siemens Krefeld 2004–05. –/60. 49.2 t.

350101	**LM**	A	*LM*	NN	63761	66811	66861	63711
350102	**LM**	A	*LM*	NN	63762	66812	66862	63712
350103	**LM**	A	*LM*	NN	63765	66813	66863	63713
350104	**LM**	A	*LM*	NN	63764	66814	66864	63714
350105	**LM**	A	*LM*	NN	63763	66815	66868	63715
350106	**LM**	A	*LM*	NN	63766	66816	66866	63716
350107	**LM**	A	*LM*	NN	63767	66817	66867	63717
350108	**LM**	A	*LM*	NN	63768	66818	66865	63718
350109	**LM**	A	*LM*	NN	63769	66819	66869	63719

350110	**AL**	A	*LM*	NN	63770	66820	66870	63720
350111	**LM**	A	*LM*	NN	63771	66821	66871	63721
350112	**LM**	A	*LM*	NN	63772	66822	66872	63722
350113	**LM**	A	*LM*	NN	63773	66823	66873	63723
350114	**LM**	A	*LM*	NN	63774	66824	66874	63724
350115	**LM**	A	*LM*	NN	63775	66825	66875	63725
350116	**LM**	A	*LM*	NN	63776	66826	66876	63726
350117	**LM**	A	*LM*	NN	63777	66827	66877	63727
350118	**LM**	A	*LM*	NN	63778	66828	66878	63728
350119	**LM**	A	*LM*	NN	63779	66829	66879	63729
350120	**LM**	A	*LM*	NN	63780	66830	66880	63730
350121	**LM**	A	*LM*	NN	63781	66831	66881	63731
350122	**LM**	A	*LM*	NN	63782	66832	66882	63732
350123	**LM**	A	*LM*	NN	63783	66833	66883	63733
350124	**LM**	A	*LM*	NN	63784	66834	66884	63734
350125	**LM**	A	*LM*	NN	63785	66835	66885	63735
350126	**LM**	A	*LM*	NN	63786	66836	66886	63736
350127	**LM**	A	*LM*	NN	63787	66837	66887	63737
350128	**LM**	A	*LM*	NN	63788	66838	66888	63738
350129	**LM**	A	*LM*	NN	63789	66839	66889	63739
350130	**LM**	A	*LM*	NN	63790	66840	66890	63740

Class 350/2. Owned by Porterbrook Leasing.

Seating Layout: 1: 2+2 facing, 2: 3+2 facing/unidirectional.

DMSO(A). Siemens Krefeld 2008–09. –/70. 43.7 t.
TCO. Siemens Prague 2008–09. 24/42 1T. 35.3 t.
PTSO. Siemens Prague 2008–09. –/61(+9) 1TD 2W. 42.9 t.
DMSO(B). Siemens Krefeld 2008–09. –/70. 44.2 t.

350231	**LM**	P	*LM*	NN	61431	65231	67531	61531
350232	**LM**	P	*LM*	NN	61432	65232	67532	61532
350233	**LM**	P	*LM*	NN	61433	65233	67533	61533
350234	**LM**	P	*LM*	NN	61434	65234	67534	61534
350235	**LM**	P	*LM*	NN	61435	65235	67535	61535
350236	**LM**	P	*LM*	NN	61436	65236	67536	61536
350237	**LM**	P	*LM*	NN	61437	65237	67537	61537
350238	**LM**	P	*LM*	NN	61438	65238	67538	61538
350239	**LM**	P	*LM*	NN	61439	65239	67539	61539
350240	**LM**	P	*LM*	NN	61440	65240	67540	61540
350241	**LM**	P	*LM*	NN	61441	65241	67541	61541
350242	**LM**	P	*LM*	NN	61442	65242	67542	61542
350243	**LM**	P	*LM*	NN	61443	65243	67543	61543
350244	**LM**	P	*LM*	NN	61444	65244	67544	61544
350245	**LM**	P	*LM*	NN	61445	65245	67545	61545
350246	**LM**	P	*LM*	NN	61446	65246	67546	61546
350247	**LM**	P	*LM*	NN	61447	65247	67547	61547
350248	**LM**	P	*LM*	NN	61448	65248	67548	61548
350249	**LM**	P	*LM*	NN	61449	65249	67549	61549
350250	**LM**	P	*LM*	NN	61450	65250	67550	61550
350251	**LM**	P	*LM*	NN	61451	65251	67551	61551
350252	**LM**	P	*LM*	NN	61452	65252	67552	61552

350 253	**LM**	P	*LM*	NN	61453	65253	67553	61553
350 254	**LM**	P	*LM*	NN	61454	65254	67554	61554
350 255	**LM**	P	*LM*	NN	61455	65255	67555	61555
350 256	**LM**	P	*LM*	NN	61456	65256	67556	61556
350 257	**LM**	P	*LM*	NN	61457	65257	67557	61557
350 258	**LM**	P	*LM*	NN	61458	65258	67558	61558
350 259	**LM**	P	*LM*	NN	61459	65259	67559	61559
350 260	**LM**	P	*LM*	NN	61460	65260	67560	61560
350 261	**LM**	P	*LM*	NN	61461	65261	67561	61561
350 262	**LM**	P	*LM*	NN	61462	65262	67562	61562
350 263	**LM**	P	*LM*	NN	61463	65263	67563	61563
350 264	**LM**	P	*LM*	NN	61464	65264	67564	61564
350 265	**LM**	P	*LM*	NN	61465	65265	67565	61565
350 266	**LM**	P	*LM*	NN	61466	65266	67566	61566
350 267	**LM**	P	*LM*	NN	61467	65267	67567	61567

Name (carried on one side of PTSO): 350 232   Chad Varah

Class 350/3. Owned by Angel Trains. London Midland units built for 110 mph operation.

Seating Layout: 1: 2+2 facing, 2: 2+2 facing/unidirectional.

DMSO(A). Siemens Krefeld 2014. –/60. 44.2 t.
TCO. Siemens Krefeld 2014. 24/36 1T. 36.3 t.
PTSO. Siemens Krefeld 2014. –/50(+9) 1TD 2W. 44.0 t.
DMSO(B). Siemens Krefeld 2014. –/60. 45.0 t.

350 368	**LM**	A	*LM*	NN	60141	60511	60651	60151
350 369	**LM**	A	*LM*	NN	60142	60512	60652	60152
350 370	**LM**	A	*LM*	NN	60143	60513	60653	60153
350 371	**LM**	A	*LM*	NN	60144	60514	60654	60154
350 372	**LM**	A	*LM*	NN	60145	60515	60655	60155
350 373	**LM**	A	*LM*	NN	60146	60516	60656	60156
350 374	**LM**	A	*LM*	NN	60147	60517	60657	60157
350 375	**LM**	A	*LM*	NN	60148	60518	60658	60158
350 376	**LM**	A	*LM*	NN	60149	60519	60659	60159
350 377	**LM**	A	*LM*	NN	60150	60520	60660	60160

Name: 350 370   Lichfield Festival

Class 350/4. Owned by Angel Trains. TransPennine Express units used on the Manchester Airport–Edinburgh/Glasgow route.

Seating Layout: 1: 2+1 facing, 2: 2+2 facing/unidirectional.

DMSO(A). Siemens Krefeld 2013–14. –/56. 44.2 t.
TCO. Siemens Krefeld 2013–14. 19/24 1T. 36.2 t.
PTSO. Siemens Krefeld 2013–14. –/42 1TD 1T. 44.6 t.
DMSO(B). Siemens Krefeld 2013–14. –/56. 45.0 t.

350 401	**FT**	A	*TP*	AK	60691	60901	60941	60671
350 402	**FT**	A	*TP*	AK	60692	60902	60942	60672
350 403	**FT**	A	*TP*	AK	60693	60903	60943	60673
350 404	**FT**	A	*TP*	AK	60694	60904	60944	60674
350 405	**FT**	A	*TP*	AK	60695	60905	60945	60675

350406	**FT**	A	*TP*	AK	60696	60906	60946	60676
350407	**FT**	A	*TP*	AK	60697	60907	60947	60677
350408	**FT**	A	*TP*	AK	60698	60908	60948	60678
350409	**FT**	A	*TP*	AK	60699	60909	60949	60679
350410	**FT**	A	*TP*	AK	60700	60910	60950	60680

CLASS 357 ELECTROSTAR
ADTRANZ/BOMBARDIER DERBY

Provision for 750 V DC supply if required.

Formation: DMSO–MSO–PTSO–DMSO.
Construction: Welded aluminium alloy underframe, sides and roof with steel ends. All sections bolted together.
Traction Motors: Two Adtranz asynchronous of 250 kW.
Wheel Arrangement: 2-Bo + 2-Bo + 2-2 + Bo-2.
Braking: Disc & regenerative.   **Dimensions:** 20.40/19.99 x 2.80 m.
Bogies: Adtranz P3-25/T3-25.   **Couplers:** Tightlock.
Gangways: Within unit.   **Control System:** IGBT Inverter.
Doors: Sliding plug.   **Maximum Speed:** 100 mph.
Heating & ventilation: Air conditioning.
Seating Layout: 3+2 facing/unidirectional.
Multiple Working: Within class.

Class 357/0. Owned by Porterbrook Leasing.

DMSO(A). Adtranz Derby 1999–2001. –/71. 40.7 t.
MSO. Adtranz Derby 1999–2001. –/78. 36.7 t.
PTSO. Adtranz Derby 1999–2001. –/58(+4) 1TD 2W. 39.5 t.
DMSO(B). Adtranz Derby 1999–2001. –/71. 40.7 t.

357001	**NC**	P	*C2*	EM	67651	74151	74051	67751
357002	**NC**	P	*C2*	EM	67652	74152	74052	67752
357003	**NC**	P	*C2*	EM	67653	74153	74053	67753
357004	**NC**	P	*C2*	EM	67654	74154	74054	67754
357005	**NC**	P	*C2*	EM	67655	74155	74055	67755
357006	**NC**	P	*C2*	EM	67656	74156	74056	67756
357007	**NC**	P	*C2*	EM	67657	74157	74057	67757
357008	**NC**	P	*C2*	EM	67658	74158	74058	67758
357009	**NC**	P	*C2*	EM	67659	74159	74059	67759
357010	**NC**	P	*C2*	EM	67660	74160	74060	67760
357011	**NC**	P	*C2*	EM	67661	74161	74061	67761
357012	**NC**	P	*C2*	EM	67662	74162	74062	67762
357013	**NC**	P	*C2*	EM	67663	74163	74063	67763
357014	**NC**	P	*C2*	EM	67664	74164	74064	67764
357015	**NC**	P	*C2*	EM	67665	74165	74065	67765
357016	**NC**	P	*C2*	EM	67666	74166	74066	67766
357017	**NC**	P	*C2*	EM	67667	74167	74067	67767
357018	**NC**	P	*C2*	EM	67668	74168	74068	67768
357019	**NC**	P	*C2*	EM	67669	74169	74069	67769
357020	**NC**	P	*C2*	EM	67670	74170	74070	67770

357 021	**NC**	P	*C2*	EM	67671	74171	74071	67771
357 022	**NC**	P	*C2*	EM	67672	74172	74072	67772
357 023	**NC**	P	*C2*	EM	67673	74173	74073	67773
357 024	**NC**	P	*C2*	EM	67674	74174	74074	67774
357 025	**NC**	P	*C2*	EM	67675	74175	74075	67775
357 026	**NC**	P	*C2*	EM	67676	74176	74076	67776
357 027	**NC**	P	*C2*	EM	67677	74177	74077	67777
357 028	**NC**	P	*C2*	EM	67678	74178	74078	67778
357 029	**NC**	P	*C2*	EM	67679	74179	74079	67779
357 030	**NC**	P	*C2*	EM	67680	74180	74080	67780
357 031	**NC**	P	*C2*	EM	67681	74181	74081	67781
357 032	**NC**	P	*C2*	EM	67682	74182	74082	67782
357 033	**NC**	P	*C2*	EM	67683	74183	74083	67783
357 034	**NC**	P	*C2*	EM	67684	74184	74084	67784
357 035	**NC**	P	*C2*	EM	67685	74185	74085	67785
357 036	**NC**	P	*C2*	EM	67686	74186	74086	67786
357 037	**NC**	P	*C2*	EM	67687	74187	74087	67787
357 038	**NC**	P	*C2*	EM	67688	74188	74088	67788
357 039	**NC**	P	*C2*	EM	67689	74189	74089	67789
357 040	**NC**	P	*C2*	EM	67690	74190	74090	67790
357 041	**NC**	P	*C2*	EM	67691	74191	74091	67791
357 042	**NC**	P	*C2*	EM	67692	74192	74092	67792
357 043	**NC**	P	*C2*	EM	67693	74193	74093	67793
357 044	**NC**	P	*C2*	EM	67694	74194	74094	67794
357 045	**NC**	P	*C2*	EM	67695	74195	74095	67795
357 046	**NC**	P	*C2*	EM	67696	74196	74096	67796

Names (carried on DMSO(A) and DMSO(B) (one plate on each)):

357 001 BARRY FLAXMAN
357 002 ARTHUR LEWIS STRIDE 1841–1922
357 003 SOUTHEND city.on.sea
357 004 TONY AMOS
357 005 SOUTHEND: 2017 Alternative City of Culture
357 006 DIAMOND JUBILEE 1952–2012
357 011 JOHN LOWING
357 028 London, Tilbury & Southend Railway 1854–2004
357 029 THOMAS WHITELEGG 1840–1922
357 030 ROBERT HARBEN WHITELEGG 1871–1957

Class 357/2. Owned by Angel Trains.

DMSO(A). Bombardier Derby 2001–02. –/71. 40.7 t.
MSO. Bombardier Derby 2001–02. –/78. 36.7 t.
PTSO. Bombardier Derby 2001–02. –/58(+4) 1TD 2W. 39.5 t.
DMSO(B). Bombardier Derby 2001–02. –/71. 40.7 t.

357 201	**NC**	A	*C2*	EM	68601	74701	74601	68701
357 202	**NC**	A	*C2*	EM	68602	74702	74602	68702
357 203	**NC**	A	*C2*	EM	68603	74703	74603	68703
357 204	**NC**	A	*C2*	EM	68604	74704	74604	68704
357 205	**NC**	A	*C2*	EM	68605	74705	74605	68705
357 206	**NC**	A	*C2*	EM	68606	74706	74606	68706

357 207	**NC**	A	*C2*	EM	68607	74707	74607	68707
357 208	**NC**	A	*C2*	EM	68608	74708	74608	68708
357 209	**NC**	A	*C2*	EM	68609	74709	74609	68709
357 210	**NC**	A	*C2*	EM	68610	74710	74610	68710
357 211	**NC**	A	*C2*	EM	68611	74711	74611	68711

Names (carried on DMSO(A) and DMSO(B) (one plate on each)):

357 201 KEN BIRD	357 206 MARTIN AUNGIER
357 202 KENNY MITCHELL	357 207 JOHN PAGE
357 203 HENRY PUMFRETT	357 208 DAVE DAVIS
357 204 DEREK FOWERS	357 209 JAMES SNELLING
357 205 JOHN D'SILVA	

Class 357/3. Owned by Angel Trains. In 2015–16 17 Class 357/2s (357 212–228) were reconfigured as "high density" units 357 312–328 with fewer seats and more standing room for shorter distance workings.

Seating Layout: 2+2 facing/unidirectional.

DMSO(A). Bombardier Derby 2001–02. –/56. 40.7 t.
MSO. Bombardier Derby 2001–02. –/50. 36.7 t.
PTSO. Bombardier Derby 2001–02. –/56(+4) 1TD 2W. 39.5 t.
DMSO(B). Bombardier Derby 2001–02. –/56. 40.7 t.

357 312	(357 212)	**NC**	A	*C2*	EM	68612	74712	74612	68712
357 313	(357 213)	**NC**	A	*C2*	EM	68613	74713	74613	68713
357 314	(357 214)	**NC**	A	*C2*	EM	68614	74714	74614	68714
357 315	(357 215)	**NC**	A	*C2*	EM	68615	74715	74615	68715
357 316	(357 216)	**NC**	A	*C2*	EM	68616	74716	74616	68716
357 317	(357 217)	**NC**	A	*C2*	EM	68617	74717	74617	68717
357 318	(357 218)	**NC**	A	*C2*	EM	68618	74718	74618	68718
357 319	(357 219)	**NC**	A	*C2*	EM	68619	74719	74619	68719
357 320	(357 220)	**NC**	A	*C2*	EM	68620	74720	74620	68720
357 321	(357 221)	**NC**	A	*C2*	EM	68621	74721	74621	68721
357 322	(357 222)	**NC**	A	*C2*	EM	68622	74722	74622	68722
357 323	(357 223)	**NC**	A	*C2*	EM	68623	74723	74623	68723
357 324	(357 224)	**NC**	A	*C2*	EM	68624	74724	74624	68724
357 325	(357 225)	**NC**	A	*C2*	EM	68625	74725	74625	68725
357 326	(357 226)	**NC**	A	*C2*	EM	68626	74726	74626	68726
357 327	(357 227)	**NC**	A	*C2*	EM	68627	74727	74627	68727
357 328	(357 228)	**NC**	A	*C2*	EM	68628	74728	74628	68728

Names (carried on DMSO(A) and DMSO(B) (one plate on each)):

357 313 UPMINSTER I.E.C.C.
357 317 ALLAN BURNELL
357 327 SOUTHEND UNITED

CLASS 360/0   DESIRO UK   SIEMENS

Outer suburban/express units.

Formation: DMCO–PTSO–TSO–DMCO.
Construction: Welded aluminium.
Traction Motors: Four Siemens 1TB2016-0GB02 asynchronous of 250 kW.
Wheel Arrangement: Bo-Bo + 2-2 + 2-2 + Bo-Bo.
Braking: Disc & regenerative.   **Dimensions:** 20.34 x 2.80 m.
Bogies: SGP SF5000.   **Couplers:** Dellner 12.
Gangways: Within unit.   **Control System:** IGBT Inverter.
Doors: Sliding plug.   **Maximum Speed:** 100 mph.
Heating & ventilation: Air conditioning.
Seating Layout: 1: 2+2 facing, 2: 3+2 facing/unidirectional.
Multiple Working: Within class.

DMCO(A). Siemens Krefeld 2002–03. 8/59. 45.0 t.
PTSO. Siemens Vienna 2002–03. –/60(+9) 1TD 2W. 43.0 t.
TSO. Siemens Vienna 2002–03. –/78. 35.0 t.
DMCO(B). Siemens Krefeld 2002–03. 8/59. 45.0 t.

360 101	**FB**	A	*GA*	IL	65551	72551	74551	68551
360 102	**FB**	A	*GA*	IL	65552	72552	74552	68552
360 103	**FB**	A	*GA*	IL	65553	72553	74553	68553
360 104	**FB**	A	*GA*	IL	65554	72554	74554	68554
360 105	**FB**	A	*GA*	IL	65555	72555	74555	68555
360 106	**FB**	A	*GA*	IL	65556	72556	74556	68556
360 107	**FB**	A	*GA*	IL	65557	72557	74557	68557
360 108	**FB**	A	*GA*	IL	65558	72558	74558	68558
360 109	**FB**	A	*GA*	IL	65559	72559	74559	68559
360 110	**FB**	A	*GA*	IL	65560	72560	74560	68560
360 111	**FB**	A	*GA*	IL	65561	72561	74561	68561
360 112	**FB**	A	*GA*	IL	65562	72562	74562	68562
360 113	**FB**	A	*GA*	IL	65563	72563	74563	68563
360 114	**FB**	A	*GA*	IL	65564	72564	74564	68564
360 115	**FB**	A	*GA*	IL	65565	72565	74565	68565
360 116	**FB**	A	*GA*	IL	65566	72566	74566	68566
360 117	**FB**	A	*GA*	IL	65567	72567	74567	68567
360 118	**FB**	A	*GA*	IL	65568	72568	74568	68568
360 119	**FB**	A	*GA*	IL	65569	72569	74569	68569
360 120	**FB**	A	*GA*	IL	65570	72570	74570	68570
360 121	**FB**	A	*GA*	IL	65571	72571	74571	68571

CLASS 360/2   DESIRO UK   SIEMENS

4-car Class 350 testbed units rebuilt for use by Heathrow Express on Paddington–Heathrow Airport stopping services ("Heathrow Connect").

Original 4-car sets 360 201–204 were made up to 5-cars during 2007 using additional TSOs. A fifth unit (360 205) was delivered in late 2005 as a 5-car set. This set is normally used on Terminals 1&3–Terminal 4 shuttle services.

Formation: DMSO–PTSO–TSO–TSO–DMSO.
Construction: Welded aluminium.
Traction Motors: Four Siemens 1TB2016-0GB02 asynchronous of 250 kW.
Wheel Arrangement: Bo-Bo + 2-2 + 2-2 + 2-2 + Bo-Bo.
Braking: Disc & regenerative.   **Dimensions:** 20.34 x 2.80 m.
Bogies: SGP SF5000.   **Couplers:** Dellner 12.
Gangways: Within unit.   **Control System:** IGBT Inverter.
Doors: Sliding plug.   **Maximum Speed:** 100 mph.
Heating & ventilation: Air conditioning.
Seating Layout: 3+2 (* 2+2) facing/unidirectional.
Multiple Working: Within class.

DMSO(A). Siemens Krefeld 2002–06. –/63 (* –/54). 44.8 t.
PTSO. Siemens Krefeld 2002–06. –/57(+9) 1TD 2W (* –/48(+9) 2W). 44.2 t.
TSO. Siemens Krefeld 2005–06. –/74 (* –/62). 35.3 t.
TSO. Siemens Krefeld 2002–06. –/74 (* –/62). 34.1 t.
DMSO(B). Siemens Krefeld 2002–06. –/63 (* –/54). 44.4 t.

360 201		HC	HE	*HC*	OH	78431	63421	72431 72421 78441
360 202		HC	HE	*HC*	OH	78432	63422	72432 72422 78442
360 203		HC	HE	*HC*	OH	78433	63423	72433 72423 78443
360 204		HC	HE	*HC*	OH	78434	63424	72434 72424 78444
360 205	*	HE	HE	*HE*	OH	78435	63425	72435 72425 78445

CLASS 365   NETWORKER EXPRESS   ABB YORK

Outer suburban units. A refurbishment programme is underway that involves fitting a new universal access toilet to comply with the 2020 accessibility regulations (units shown *).

Formations: DMCO–TSO–PTSO–DMCO.
Systems: 25 kV AC overhead but with 750 V DC third rail capability (units 365 501–516 were formerly used on DC lines in the South-East).
Construction: Welded aluminium alloy.
Traction Motors: Four GEC-Alsthom G354CX asynchronous of 157 kW.
Wheel Arrangement: Bo-Bo + 2-2 + 2-2 + Bo-Bo.
Braking: Disc & rheostatic.   **Dimensions:** 20.89/20.06 x 2.81 m.
Bogies: ABB P3-16/T3-16.   **Couplers:** Tightlock.
Gangways: Within unit.   **Control System:** GTO Inverter.
Doors: Sliding plug.   **Maximum Speed:** 100 mph.
Seating Layout: 1: 2+2 facing, 2: 2+2 facing.
Multiple Working: Within class only.

DMCO(A). Lot No. 31133 1994–95. 12/56. 41.7 t.
TSO. Lot No. 31134 1994–95. –/65 1TD (* –/58 1TD 2W) 32.9 t.
PTSO. Lot No. 31135 1994–95. –/68 1T (* –/70 1T). 35.2 t.
DMCO(B). Lot No. 31136 1994–95. 12/56. 41.7 t.

365 501	*	TL	E	GN	HE	65894	72241	72240	65935
365 502	*	TL	E	GN	HE	65895	72243	72242	65936
365 503	*	TL	E	GN	HE	65896	72245	72244	65937
365 504	*	TL	E	GN	HE	65897	72247	72246	65938
365 505	*	TL	E	GN	HE	65898	72249	72248	65939
365 506	*	TL	E	GN	HE	65899	72251	72250	65940
365 507	*	TL	E	GN	HE	65900	72253	72252	65941
365 508	*	TL	E	GN	HE	65901	72255	72254	65942
365 509	*	TL	E	GN	HE	65902	72257	72256	65943
365 510	*	TL	E	GN	HE	65903	72259	72258	65944
365 511	*	TL	E	GN	HE	65904	72261	72260	65945
365 512	*	TL	E	GN	HE	65905	72263	72262	65946
365 513	*	TL	E	GN	HE	65906	72265	72264	65947
365 514	*	TL	E	GN	HE	65907	72267	72266	65948
365 515	*	TL	E	GN	HE	65908	72269	72268	65949
365 516	*	TL	E	GN	HE	65909	72271	72270	65950
365 517		TL	E	GN	HE	65910	72273	72272	65951
365 518	*	TL	E	GN	HE	65911	72275	72274	65952
365 519	*	TL	E	GN	HE	65912	72277	72276	65953
365 520		TL	E	GN	HE	65913	72279	72278	65954
365 521	*	TL	E	GN	HE	65914	72281	72280	65955
365 522		TL	E	GN	HE	65915	72283	72282	65956
365 523		TL	E	GN	HE	65916	72285	72284	65957
365 524		TL	E	GN	HE	65917	72287	72286	65958
365 525		TL	E	GN	HE	65918	72289	72288	65959
365 527	*	TL	E	GN	HE	65920	72293	72292	65961
365 528		TL	E	GN	HE	65921	72295	72294	65962
365 529	*	TL	E	GN	HE	65922	72297	72296	65963
365 530	*	TL	E	GN	HE	65923	72299	72298	65964
365 531	*	TL	E	GN	HE	65924	72301	72300	65965
365 532	*	TL	E	GN	HE	65925	72303	72302	65966
365 533		TL	E	GN	HE	65926	72305	72304	65967
365 534	*	TL	E	GN	HE	65927	72307	72306	65968
365 535	*	TL	E	GN	HE	65928	72309	72308	65969
365 536	*	TL	E	GN	HE	65929	72311	72310	65970
365 537	*	TL	E	GN	HE	65930	72313	72312	65971
365 538		TL	E	GN	HE	65931	72315	72314	65972
365 539	*	TL	E	GN	HE	65932	72317	72316	65973
365 540		TL	E	GN	HE	65933	72319	72318	65974
365 541	*	TL	E	GN	HE	65934	72321	72320	65975

Names (carried on each DMCO):

365 517 Supporting Red Balloon
365 533 Max Appeal
365 537 Daniel Edwards (1974–2010) Cambridge Driver

CLASS 375 ELECTROSTAR
ADTRANZ/BOMBARDIER DERBY

Express and outer suburban units.

Formations: Various.
Systems: 25 kV AC overhead/750 V DC third rail (some third rail only with provision for retro-fitting of AC equipment).
Construction: Welded aluminium alloy underframe, sides and roof with steel ends. All sections bolted together.
Traction Motors: Two Adtranz asynchronous of 250 kW.
Wheel Arrangement: 2-Bo (+ 2-Bo) + 2-2 + Bo-2.
Braking: Disc & regenerative.   **Dimensions:** 20.40/19.99 x 2.80 m.
Bogies: Adtranz P3-25/T3-25.   **Couplers:** Dellner 12.
Gangways: Throughout.   **Control System:** IGBT Inverter.
Doors: Sliding plug.   **Maximum Speed:** 100 mph.
Heating & ventilation: Air conditioning.
Seating Layout: 1: 2+2 facing/unidirectional. 2: 2+2 facing/unidirectional (except 375/9 – 3+2 facing/unidirectional).
Multiple Working: Within class and with Classes 376, 377, 378 and 379.

Class 375/3. Express units. 750 V DC only. DMSO–TSO–DMCO.

DMSO. Bombardier Derby 2001–02. –/60. 43.8 t.
TSO. Bombardier Derby 2001–02. –/56 1TD 2W. 35.5 t.
DMCO. Bombardier Derby 2001–02. 12/48. 43.8 t.

375301	SB	E	SE	RM	67921	74351	67931
375302	SB	E	SE	RM	67922	74352	67932
375303	SB	E	SE	RM	67923	74353	67933
375304	SB	E	SE	RM	67924	74354	67934
375305	SB	E	SE	RM	67925	74355	67935
375306	SB	E	SE	RM	67926	74356	67936
375307	SB	E	SE	RM	67927	74357	67937
375308	SB	E	SE	RM	67928	74358	67938
375309	SB	E	SE	RM	67929	74359	67939
375310	SB	E	SE	RM	67930	74360	67940

Class 375/6. Express units. 25 kV AC/750 V DC. DMCO–MSO–PTSO–DMCO († refurbished – DMSO–MCO–PTSO–DMSO).

DMCO(A). Adtranz Derby 1999–2001. –/60. 46.2 t.
MSO. Adtranz Derby 1999–2001. 16/50 1T. 40.5 t.
PTSO. Adtranz Derby 1999–2001. –/56 1TD 2W. 40.7 t.
DMCO(B). Adtranz Derby 1999–2001. –/60. 46.2 t.

375601	SB	E	SE	RM	67801	74251	74201	67851
375602	SB	E	SE	RM	67802	74252	74202	67852
375603	SB	E	SE	RM	67803	74253	74203	67853
375604	SB	E	SE	RM	67804	74254	74204	67854
375605	SB	E	SE	RM	67805	74255	74205	67855
375606	SB	E	SE	RM	67806	74256	74206	67856
375607	SB	E	SE	RM	67807	74257	74207	67857

375608	**SB**	E	*SE*	RM	67808	74258	74208	67858
375609	**SB**	E	*SE*	RM	67809	74259	74209	67859
375610	**SB**	E	*SE*	RM	67810	74260	74210	67860
375611	**SB**	E	*SE*	RM	67811	74261	74211	67861
375612	**SB**	E	*SE*	RM	67812	74262	74212	67862
375613	**SB**	E	*SE*	RM	67813	74263	74213	67863
375614	**SB**	E	*SE*	RM	67814	74264	74214	67864
375615	**SB**	E	*SE*	RM	67815	74265	74215	67865
375616	**SB**	E	*SE*	RM	67816	74266	74216	67866
375617	**SB**	E	*SE*	RM	67817	74267	74217	67867
375618	**SB**	E	*SE*	RM	67818	74268	74218	67868
375619	**SB**	E	*SE*	RM	67819	74269	74219	67869
375620	**SB**	E	*SE*	RM	67820	74270	74220	67870
375621	**SB**	E	*SE*	RM	67821	74271	74221	67871
375622	**SB**	E	*SE*	RM	67822	74272	74222	67872
375623	**SB**	E	*SE*	RM	67823	74273	74223	67873
375624	**SB**	E	*SE*	RM	67824	74274	74224	67874
375625	**SB**	E	*SE*	RM	67825	74275	74225	67875
375626	**SB**	E	*SE*	RM	67826	74276	74226	67876
375627	**SB**	E	*SE*	RM	67827	74277	74227	67877
375628	**SB**	E	*SE*	RM	67828	74278	74228	67878
375629	**SB**	E	*SE*	RM	67829	74279	74229	67879
375630	**SB**	E	*SE*	RM	67830	74280	74230	67880

Class 375/7. Express units. 750 V DC only. DMCO–MSO–TSO–DMCO.

DMCO(A). Bombardier Derby 2001–02. –/60. 43.8 t.
MSO. Bombardier Derby 2001–02. 16/50 1T. 36.4 t.
TSO. Bombardier Derby 2001–02. –/56 1TD 2W. 34.1 t.
DMCO(B). Bombardier Derby 2001–02. –/60. 43.8 t.

375701	**SB**	E	*SE*	RM	67831	74281	74231	67881
375702	**SB**	E	*SE*	RM	67832	74282	74232	67882
375703	**SB**	E	*SE*	RM	67833	74283	74233	67883
375704	**SB**	E	*SE*	RM	67834	74284	74234	67884
375705	**SB**	E	*SE*	RM	67835	74285	74235	67885
375706	**SB**	E	*SE*	RM	67836	74286	74236	67886
375707	**SB**	E	*SE*	RM	67837	74287	74237	67887
375708	**SB**	E	*SE*	RM	67838	74288	74238	67888
375709	**SB**	E	*SE*	RM	67839	74289	74239	67889
375710	**SB**	E	*SE*	RM	67840	74290	74240	67890
375711	**SB**	E	*SE*	RM	67841	74291	74241	67891
375712	**SB**	E	*SE*	RM	67842	74292	74242	67892
375713	**SB**	E	*SE*	RM	67843	74293	74243	67893
375714	**SB**	E	*SE*	RM	67844	74294	74244	67894
375715	**SB**	E	*SE*	RM	67845	74295	74245	67895

Names (carried on one side of each MSO or TSO):

375710 Rochester Castle
375714 Rochester Cathedral

Class 375/8. Express units. 750 V DC only. DMCO–MSO–TSO–DMCO.

375 801–820 are fitted with de-icing equipment. TSO weighs 36.5 t.

DMCO(A). Bombardier Derby 2004. 12/48. 43.3 t.
MSO. Bombardier Derby 2004. –/66 1T. 39.8 t.
TSO. Bombardier Derby 2004. –/52 1TD 2W. 35.9 t.
DMCO(B). Bombardier Derby 2004. 12/52. 43.3 t.

375801	**CN**	E	*SE*	RM	73301	79001	78201	73701
375802	**CN**	E	*SE*	RM	73302	79002	78202	73702
375803	**CN**	E	*SE*	RM	73303	79003	78203	73703
375804	**CN**	E	*SE*	RM	73304	79004	78204	73704
375805	**CN**	E	*SE*	RM	73305	79005	78205	73705
375806	**CN**	E	*SE*	RM	73306	79006	78206	73706
375807	**CN**	E	*SE*	RM	73307	79007	78207	73707
375808	**CN**	E	*SE*	RM	73308	79008	78208	73708
375809	**CN**	E	*SE*	RM	73309	79009	78209	73709
375810	**CN**	E	*SE*	RM	73310	79010	78210	73710
375811	**CN**	E	*SE*	RM	73311	79011	78211	73711
375812	**CN**	E	*SE*	RM	73312	79012	78212	73712
375813	**CN**	E	*SE*	RM	73313	79013	78213	73713
375814	**CN**	E	*SE*	RM	73314	79014	78214	73714
375815	**CN**	E	*SE*	RM	73315	79015	78215	73715
375816	**CN**	E	*SE*	RM	73316	79016	78216	73716
375817	**CN**	E	*SE*	RM	73317	79017	78217	73717
375818	**CN**	E	*SE*	RM	73318	79018	78218	73718
375819	**CN**	E	*SE*	RM	73319	79019	78219	73719
375820	**CN**	E	*SE*	RM	73320	79020	78220	73720
375821	**CN**	E	*SE*	RM	73321	79021	78221	73721
375822	**CN**	E	*SE*	RM	73322	79022	78222	73722
375823	**CN**	E	*SE*	RM	73323	79023	78223	73723
375824	**CN**	E	*SE*	RM	73324	79024	78224	73724
375825	**CN**	E	*SE*	RM	73325	79025	78225	73725
375826	**CN**	E	*SE*	RM	73326	79026	78226	73726
375827	**CN**	E	*SE*	RM	73327	79027	78227	73727
375828	**CN**	E	*SE*	RM	73328	79028	78228	73728
375829	**CN**	E	*SE*	RM	73329	79029	78229	73729
375830	**CN**	E	*SE*	RM	73330	79030	78230	73730

Name (carried on one side of each MSO or TSO):

375830 City of London

Class 375/9. Outer suburban units. 750 V DC only. DMCO–MSO–TSO–DMCO.

DMCO(A). Bombardier Derby 2003–04. 12/59. 43.4 t.
MSO. Bombardier Derby 2003–04. –/73 1T. 39.3 t.
TSO. Bombardier Derby 2003–04. –/59 1TD 2W. 35.6 t.
DMCO(B). Bombardier Derby 2003–04. 12/59. 43.4 t.

375901	**CN**	E	*SE*	RM	73331	79031	79061	73731
375902	**CN**	E	*SE*	RM	73332	79032	79062	73732
375903	**CN**	E	*SE*	RM	73333	79033	79063	73733
375904	**CN**	E	*SE*	RM	73334	79034	79064	73734

375905	**CN**	E	*SE*	RM	73335	79035	79065	73735
375906	**CN**	E	*SE*	RM	73336	79036	79066	73736
375907	**CN**	E	*SE*	RM	73337	79037	79067	73737
375908	**CN**	E	*SE*	RM	73338	79038	79068	73738
375909	**CN**	E	*SE*	RM	73339	79039	79069	73739
375910	**CN**	E	*SE*	RM	73340	79040	79070	73740
375911	**CN**	E	*SE*	RM	73341	79041	79071	73741
375912	**CN**	E	*SE*	RM	73342	79042	79072	73742
375913	**CN**	E	*SE*	RM	73343	79043	79073	73743
375914	**CN**	E	*SE*	RM	73344	79044	79074	73744
375915	**CN**	E	*SE*	RM	73345	79045	79075	73745
375916	**CN**	E	*SE*	RM	73346	79046	79076	73746
375917	**CN**	E	*SE*	RM	73347	79047	79077	73747
375918	**CN**	E	*SE*	RM	73348	79048	79078	73748
375919	**CN**	E	*SE*	RM	73349	79049	79079	73749
375920	**CN**	E	*SE*	RM	73350	79050	79080	73750
375921	**CN**	E	*SE*	RM	73351	79051	79081	73751
375922	**CN**	E	*SE*	RM	73352	79052	79082	73752
375923	**CN**	E	*SE*	RM	73353	79053	79083	73753
375924	**CN**	E	*SE*	RM	73354	79054	79084	73754
375925	**CN**	E	*SE*	RM	73355	79055	79085	73755
375926	**CN**	E	*SE*	RM	73356	79056	79086	73756
375927	**CN**	E	*SE*	RM	73357	79057	79087	73757

CLASS 376   ELECTROSTAR   BOMBARDIER DERBY

Inner suburban units.

Formation: DMSO–MSO–TSO–MSO–DMSO.
System: 750 V DC third rail.
Construction: Welded aluminium alloy underframe, sides and roof with steel ends. All sections bolted together.
Traction Motors: Two Bombardier asynchronous of 200 kW.
Wheel Arrangement: 2-Bo + 2-Bo + 2-2 + Bo-2 + Bo-2.
Braking: Disc & regenerative.   **Dimensions:** 20.40/19.99 x 2.80 m.
Bogies: Bombardier P3-25/T3-25.   **Couplers:** Dellner 12.
Gangways: Within unit.   **Control System:** IGBT Inverter.
Doors: Sliding.   **Maximum Speed:** 75 mph.
Heating & ventilation: Pressure heating and ventilation.
Seating Layout: 2+2 low density facing.
Multiple Working: Within class and with Classes 375, 377, 378 and 379.

DMSO(A). Bombardier Derby 2004–05. –/36(+6) 1W. 42.1 t.
MSO. Bombardier Derby 2004–05. –/48. 36.2 t.
TSO. Bombardier Derby 2004–05. –/48. 36.3 t.
DMSO(B). Bombardier Derby 2004–05. –/36(+6) 1W. 42.1 t.

376001	**CN**	E	*SE*	SG	61101	63301	64301	63501	61601
376002	**CN**	E	*SE*	SG	61102	63302	64302	63502	61602
376003	**CN**	E	*SE*	SG	61103	63303	64303	63503	61603
376004	**CN**	E	*SE*	SG	61104	63304	64304	63504	61604
376005	**CN**	E	*SE*	SG	61105	63305	64305	63505	61605

376006	CN	E	SE	SG	61106 63306 64306 63506 61606
376007	CN	E	SE	SG	61107 63307 64307 63507 61607
376008	CN	E	SE	SG	61108 63308 64308 63508 61608
376009	CN	E	SE	SG	61109 63309 64309 63509 61609
376010	CN	E	SE	SG	61110 63310 64310 63510 61610
376011	CN	E	SE	SG	61111 63311 64311 63511 61611
376012	CN	E	SE	SG	61112 63312 64312 63512 61612
376013	CN	E	SE	SG	61113 63313 64313 63513 61613
376014	CN	E	SE	SG	61114 63314 64314 63514 61614
376015	CN	E	SE	SG	61115 63315 64315 63515 61615
376016	CN	E	SE	SG	61116 63316 64316 63516 61616
376017	CN	E	SE	SG	61117 63317 64317 63517 61617
376018	CN	E	SE	SG	61118 63318 64318 63518 61618
376019	CN	E	SE	SG	61119 63319 64319 63519 61619
376020	CN	E	SE	SG	61120 63320 64320 63520 61620
376021	CN	E	SE	SG	61121 63321 64321 63521 61621
376022	CN	E	SE	SG	61122 63322 64322 63522 61622
376023	CN	E	SE	SG	61123 63323 64323 63523 61623
376024	CN	E	SE	SG	61124 63324 64324 63524 61624
376025	CN	E	SE	SG	61125 63325 64325 63525 61625
376026	CN	E	SE	SG	61126 63326 64326 63526 61626
376027	CN	E	SE	SG	61127 63327 64327 63527 61627
376028	CN	E	SE	SG	61128 63328 64328 63528 61628
376029	CN	E	SE	SG	61129 63329 64329 63529 61629
376030	CN	E	SE	SG	61130 63330 64330 63530 61630
376031	CN	E	SE	SG	61131 63331 64331 63531 61631
376032	CN	E	SE	SG	61132 63332 64332 63532 61632
376033	CN	E	SE	SG	61133 63333 64333 63533 61633
376034	CN	E	SE	SG	61134 63334 64334 63534 61634
376035	CN	E	SE	SG	61135 63335 64335 63535 61635
376036	CN	E	SE	SG	61136 63336 64336 63536 61636

CLASS 377   ELECTROSTAR   BOMBARDIER DERBY

Express and outer suburban units.

Formations: Various.
Systems: 25 kV AC overhead/750 V DC third rail or third rail only with provision for retro-fitting of AC equipment.
Construction: Welded aluminium alloy underframe, sides and roof with steel ends. All sections bolted together.
Traction Motors: Two Bombardier asynchronous of 250 kW.
Wheel Arrangement: 2-Bo + 2-2 + Bo-2 or 2-Bo + 2-Bo + 2-2 + Bo-2 or 2-Bo + 2-Bo + 2-2 + Bo-2 + Bo-2.
Braking: Disc & regenerative.
Bogies: Bombardier P3-25/T3-25.
Gangways: Throughout.
Doors: Sliding plug.
Heating & ventilation: Air conditioning.
Seating Layout: Various, see sub-class headings.
Dimensions: 20.39/20.00 x 2.80 m.
Couplers: Dellner 12.
Control System: IGBT Inverter.
Maximum Speed: 100 mph.
Multiple Working: Within class and with Classes 375, 376, 378, 379 and 387.

Class 377/1. 750 V DC only. DMCO–MSO–TSO–DMCO.
Seating layout: 1: 2+2 facing/unidirectional, 2: 2+2 facing/unidirectional (377 101–119), 3+2/2+2 facing/unidirectional (377 120–139), 3+2 (middle cars and 2+2 (end cars) facing/unidirectional (377 140–164).

DMCO(A). Bombardier Derby 2002–03. 12/48 (s 12/56). 44.8 t.
MSO. Bombardier Derby 2002–03. –/62 (s –/70, t –/69). 1T. 39.0 t.
TSO. Bombardier Derby 2002–03. –/52 (s –/60, t –/57). 1TD 2W. 35.4 t.
DMCO(B). Bombardier Derby 2002–03. 12/48 (s 12/56). 43.4 t.

377 101		**SN**	P	*SN*	BI	78501	77101	78901	78701
377 102		**SN**	P	*SN*	BI	78502	77102	78902	78702
377 103		**SN**	P	*SN*	BI	78503	77103	78903	78703
377 104		**SN**	P	*SN*	BI	78504	77104	78904	78704
377 105		**SN**	P	*SN*	BI	78505	77105	78905	78705
377 106		**SN**	P	*SN*	BI	78506	77106	78906	78706
377 107		**SN**	P	*SN*	BI	78507	77107	78907	78707
377 108		**SN**	P	*SN*	BI	78508	77108	78908	78708
377 109		**SN**	P	*SN*	BI	78509	77109	78909	78709
377 110		**SN**	P	*SN*	BI	78510	77110	78910	78710
377 111		**SN**	P	*SN*	BI	78511	77111	78911	78711
377 112		**SN**	P	*SN*	BI	78512	77112	78912	78712
377 113		**SN**	P	*SN*	BI	78513	77113	78913	78713
377 114		**SN**	P	*SN*	BI	78514	77114	78914	78714
377 115		**SN**	P	*SN*	BI	78515	77115	78915	78715
377 116		**SN**	P	*SN*	BI	78516	77116	78916	78716
377 117		**SN**	P	*SN*	BI	78517	77117	78917	78717
377 118		**SN**	P	*SN*	BI	78518	77118	78918	78718
377 119		**SN**	P	*SN*	BI	78519	77119	78919	78719
377 120	s	**SN**	P	*SN*	BI	78520	77120	78920	78720
377 121	s	**SN**	P	*SN*	BI	78521	77121	78921	78721
377 122	s	**SN**	P	*SN*	BI	78522	77122	78922	78722
377 123	s	**SN**	P	*SN*	BI	78523	77123	78923	78723
377 124	s	**SN**	P	*SN*	BI	78524	77124	78924	78724
377 125	s	**SN**	P	*SN*	BI	78525	77125	78925	78725
377 126	s	**SN**	P	*SN*	BI	78526	77126	78926	78726
377 127	s	**SN**	P	*SN*	BI	78527	77127	78927	78727
377 128	s	**SN**	P	*SN*	BI	78528	77128	78928	78728
377 129	s	**SN**	P	*SN*	BI	78529	77129	78929	78729
377 130	s	**SN**	P	*SN*	BI	78530	77130	78930	78730
377 131	s	**SN**	P	*SN*	BI	78531	77131	78931	78731
377 132	s	**SN**	P	*SN*	BI	78532	77132	78932	78732
377 133	s	**SN**	P	*SN*	BI	78533	77133	78933	78733
377 134	s	**SN**	P	*SN*	BI	78534	77134	78934	78734
377 135	s	**SN**	P	*SN*	BI	78535	77135	78935	78735
377 136	s	**SN**	P	*SN*	BI	78536	77136	78936	78736
377 137	s	**SN**	P	*SN*	BI	78537	77137	78937	78737
377 138	s	**SN**	P	*SN*	BI	78538	77138	78938	78738
377 139	s	**SN**	P	*SN*	BI	78539	77139	78939	78739
377 140	t	**SN**	P	*SN*	BI	78540	77140	78940	78740
377 141	t	**SN**	P	*SN*	BI	78541	77141	78941	78741
377 142	t	**SN**	P	*SN*	BI	78542	77142	78942	78742

377 143	t	**SN**	P	*SN*	BI	78543	77143	78943	78743
377 144	t	**SN**	P	*SN*	BI	78544	77144	78944	78744
377 145	t	**SN**	P	*SN*	BI	78545	77145	78945	78745
377 146	t	**SN**	P	*SN*	BI	78546	77146	78946	78746
377 147	t	**SN**	P	*SN*	BI	78547	77147	78947	78747
377 148	t	**SN**	P	*SN*	BI	78548	77148	78948	78748
377 149	t	**SN**	P	*SN*	BI	78549	77149	78949	78749
377 150	t	**SN**	P	*SN*	BI	78550	77150	78950	78750
377 151	t	**SN**	P	*SN*	BI	78551	77151	78951	78751
377 152	t	**SN**	P	*SN*	BI	78552	77152	78952	78752
377 153	t	**SN**	P	*SN*	BI	78553	77153	78953	78753
377 154	t	**SN**	P	*SN*	BI	78554	77154	78954	78754
377 155	t	**SN**	P	*SN*	BI	78555	77155	78955	78755
377 156	t	**SN**	P	*SN*	BI	78556	77156	78956	78756
377 157	t	**SN**	P	*SN*	BI	78557	77157	78957	78757
377 158	t	**SN**	P	*SN*	BI	78558	77158	78958	78758
377 159	t	**SN**	P	*SN*	BI	78559	77159	78959	78759
377 160	t	**SN**	P	*SN*	BI	78560	77160	78960	78760
377 161	t	**SN**	P	*SN*	BI	78561	77161	78961	78761
377 162	t	**SN**	P	*SN*	BI	78562	77162	78962	78762
377 163	t	**SN**	P	*SN*	BI	78563	77163	78963	78763
377 164	t	**SN**	P	*SN*	BI	78564	77164	78964	78764

Class 377/2. 25 kV AC/750 V DC. DMCO–MSO–PTSO–DMCO. Dual-voltage units. **Seating layout:** 1: 2+2 facing/unidirectional, 2: 2+2 and 3+2 facing/unidirectional (3+2 seating in middle cars only).

DMCO(A). Bombardier Derby 2003–04. 12/48. 44.2 t.
MSO. Bombardier Derby 2003–04. –/69 1T. 39.8 t.
PTSO. Bombardier Derby 2003–04. –/57 1TD 2W. 40.1 t.
DMCO(B). Bombardier Derby 2003–04. 12/48. 44.2 t.

377 201	**SN**	P	*SN*	SU	78571	77171	78971	78771
377 202	**SN**	P	*SN*	SU	78572	77172	78972	78772
377 203	**SN**	P	*SN*	SU	78573	77173	78973	78773
377 204	**SN**	P	*SN*	SU	78574	77174	78974	78774
377 205	**SN**	P	*SN*	SU	78575	77175	78975	78775
377 206	**SN**	P	*SN*	SU	78576	77176	78976	78776
377 207	**FU**	P	*TL*	BF	78577	77177	78977	78777
377 208	**SN**	P	*TL*	BF	78578	77178	78978	78778
377 209	**SN**	P	*TL*	BF	78579	77179	78979	78779
377 210	**SN**	P	*TL*	BF	78580	77180	78980	78780
377 211	**FU**	P	*TL*	BF	78581	77181	78981	78781
377 212	**FU**	P	*TL*	BF	78582	77182	78982	78782
377 213	**SN**	P	*TL*	BF	78583	77183	78983	78783
377 214	**SN**	P	*TL*	BF	78584	77184	78984	78784
377 215	**SN**	P	*TL*	BF	78585	77185	78985	78785

Class 377/3. 750 V DC only. DMCO–TSO–DMCO.
Seating Layout: 1: 2+2 facing/unidirectional, 2: 2+2 facing/unidirectional.

Units built as Class 375, but renumbered in the Class 377/3 range when fitted with Dellner couplers.

DMCO(A). Bombardier Derby 2001–02. 12/48. 43.5 t.
TSO. Bombardier Derby 2001–02. –/56 1TD 2W. 35.4 t.
DMCO(B). Bombardier Derby 2001–02. 12/48. 43.5 t.

377 301	(375 311)	**SN**	P	*SN*	SU	68201	74801	68401
377 302	(375 312)	**SN**	P	*SN*	SU	68202	74802	68402
377 303	(375 313)	**SN**	P	*SN*	SU	68203	74803	68403
377 304	(375 314)	**SN**	P	*SN*	SU	68204	74804	68404
377 305	(375 315)	**SN**	P	*SN*	SU	68205	74805	68405
377 306	(375 316)	**SN**	P	*SN*	SU	68206	74806	68406
377 307	(375 317)	**SN**	P	*SN*	SU	68207	74807	68407
377 308	(375 318)	**SN**	P	*SN*	SU	68208	74808	68408
377 309	(375 319)	**SN**	P	*SN*	SU	68209	74809	68409
377 310	(375 320)	**SN**	P	*SN*	SU	68210	74810	68410
377 311	(375 321)	**SN**	P	*SN*	SU	68211	74811	68411
377 312	(375 322)	**SN**	P	*SN*	SU	68212	74812	68412
377 313	(375 323)	**SN**	P	*SN*	SU	68213	74813	68413
377 314	(375 324)	**SN**	P	*SN*	SU	68214	74814	68414
377 315	(375 325)	**SN**	P	*SN*	SU	68215	74815	68415
377 316	(375 326)	**SN**	P	*SN*	SU	68216	74816	68416
377 317	(375 327)	**SN**	P	*SN*	SU	68217	74817	68417
377 318	(375 328)	**SN**	P	*SN*	SU	68218	74818	68418
377 319	(375 329)	**SN**	P	*SN*	SU	68219	74819	68419
377 320	(375 330)	**SN**	P	*SN*	SU	68220	74820	68420
377 321	(375 331)	**SN**	P	*SN*	SU	68221	74821	68421
377 322	(375 332)	**SN**	P	*SN*	SU	68222	74822	68422
377 323	(375 333)	**SN**	P	*SN*	SU	68223	74823	68423
377 324	(375 334)	**SN**	P	*SN*	SU	68224	74824	68424
377 325	(375 335)	**SN**	P	*SN*	SU	68225	74825	68425
377 326	(375 336)	**SN**	P	*SN*	SU	68226	74826	68426
377 327	(375 337)	**SN**	P	*SN*	SU	68227	74827	68427
377 328	(375 338)	**SN**	P	*SN*	SU	68228	74828	68428

Class 377/4. 750 V DC only. DMCO–MSO–TSO–DMCO.
Seating Layout: 1: 2+2 facing/two seats longitudinal, 2: 2+2 and 3+2 facing/unidirectional (3+2 seating in middle cars only).

DMCO(A). Bombardier Derby 2004–05. 10/48. 43.1 t.
MSO. Bombardier Derby 2004–05. –/69 1T. 39.3 t.
TSO. Bombardier Derby 2004–05. –/56 1TD 2W. 35.3 t.
DMCO(B). Bombardier Derby 2004–05. 10/48. 43.2 t.

377 401	**SN**	P	*SN*	BI	73401	78801	78601	73801
377 402	**SN**	P	*SN*	BI	73402	78802	78602	73802
377 403	**SN**	P	*SN*	BI	73403	78803	78603	73803
377 404	**SN**	P	*SN*	BI	73404	78804	78604	73804
377 405	**SN**	P	*SN*	BI	73405	78805	78605	73805
377 406	**SN**	P	*SN*	BI	73406	78806	78606	73806
377 407	**SN**	P	*SN*	BI	73407	78807	78607	73807
377 408	**SN**	P	*SN*	BI	73408	78808	78608	73808
377 409	**SN**	P	*SN*	BI	73409	78809	78609	73809
377 410	**SN**	P	*SN*	BI	73410	78810	78610	73810
377 411	**SN**	P	*SN*	BI	73411	78811	78611	73811

377 412	**SN**	P	*SN*	BI	73412	78812	78612	73812
377 413	**SN**	P	*SN*	BI	73413	78813	78613	73813
377 414	**SN**	P	*SN*	BI	73414	78814	78614	73814
377 415	**SN**	P	*SN*	BI	73415	78815	78615	73815
377 416	**SN**	P	*SN*	BI	73416	78816	78616	73816
377 417	**SN**	P	*SN*	BI	73417	78817	78617	73817
377 418	**SN**	P	*SN*	BI	73418	78818	78618	73818
377 419	**SN**	P	*SN*	BI	73419	78819	78619	73819
377 420	**SN**	P	*SN*	BI	73420	78820	78620	73820
377 421	**SN**	P	*SN*	BI	73421	78821	78621	73821
377 422	**SN**	P	*SN*	BI	73422	78822	78622	73822
377 423	**SN**	P	*SN*	BI	73423	78823	78623	73823
377 424	**SN**	P	*SN*	BI	73424	78824	78624	73824
377 425	**SN**	P	*SN*	BI	73425	78825	78625	73825
377 426	**SN**	P	*SN*	BI	73426	78826	78626	73826
377 427	**SN**	P	*SN*	BI	73427	78827	78627	73827
377 428	**SN**	P	*SN*	BI	73428	78828	78628	73828
377 429	**SN**	P	*SN*	BI	73429	78829	78629	73829
377 430	**SN**	P	*SN*	BI	73430	78830	78630	73830
377 431	**SN**	P	*SN*	BI	73431	78831	78631	73831
377 432	**SN**	P	*SN*	BI	73432	78832	78632	73832
377 433	**SN**	P	*SN*	BI	73433	78833	78633	73833
377 434	**SN**	P	*SN*	BI	73434	78834	78634	73834
377 435	**SN**	P	*SN*	BI	73435	78835	78635	73835
377 436	**SN**	P	*SN*	BI	73436	78836	78636	73836
377 437	**SN**	P	*SN*	BI	73437	78837	78637	73837
377 438	**SN**	P	*SN*	BI	73438	78838	78638	73838
377 439	**SN**	P	*SN*	BI	73439	78839	78639	73839
377 440	**SN**	P	*SN*	BI	73440	78840	78640	73840
377 441	**SN**	P	*SN*	BI	73441	78841	78641	73841
377 442	**SN**	P	*SN*	BI	73442	78842	78642	73842
377 443	**SN**	P	*SN*	BI	73443	78843	78643	73843
377 444	**SN**	P	*SN*	BI	73444	78844	78644	73844
377 445	**SN**	P	*SN*	BI	73445	78845	78645	73845
377 446	**SN**	P	*SN*	BI	73446	78846	78646	73846
377 447	**SN**	P	*SN*	BI	73447	78847	78647	73847
377 448	**SN**	P	*SN*	BI	73448	78848	78648	73848
377 449	**SN**	P	*SN*	BI	73449	78849	78649	73849
377 450	**SN**	P	*SN*	BI	73450	78850	78650	73850
377 451	**SN**	P	*SN*	BI	73451	78851	78651	73851
377 452	**SN**	P	*SN*	BI	73452	78852	78652	73852
377 453	**SN**	P	*SN*	BI	73453	78853	78653	73853
377 454	**SN**	P	*SN*	BI	73454	78854	78654	73854
377 455	**SN**	P	*SN*	BI	73455	78855	78655	73855
377 456	**SN**	P	*SN*	BI	73456	78856	78656	73856
377 457	**SN**	P	*SN*	BI	73457	78857	78657	73857
377 458	**SN**	P	*SN*	BI	73458	78858	78658	73858
377 459	**SN**	P	*SN*	BI	73459	78859	78659	73859
377 460	**SN**	P	*SN*	BI	73460	78860	78660	73860
377 461	**SN**	P	*SN*	BI	73461	78861	78661	73861
377 462	**SN**	P	*SN*	BI	73462	78862	78662	73862

▲ Southern-liveried 313 204 leaves Lewes with the 14.17 Brighton–Seaford on 01/02/15.　　　**Robert Pritchard**

▼ Still in Strathclyde PTE livery, 314 206 is seen on the outskirts of Neilston with the 12.30 Neilston–Glasgow Central on 10/05/16.　　　**Stuart Fowler**

▲ London Overground-liveried 317 714 leads the 16.40 Chingford–London Liverpool Street through Hackney Central on 09/06/16. **Antony Guppy**

▼ Thameslink-liveried 319 444 arrives at Luton with the 16.37 from Sutton on 28/07/16. **Robert Pritchard**

▲ ScotRail Saltire-liveried 320 417 and 320 415 (both renumbered 321/4s) approach Lanark with the 16.50 from Glasgow Central on 26/08/16. **Robin Ralston**

▼ London Midland-liveried 323 243 calls at Tipton with the 12.20 Wolverhampton–Walsall on 14/03/16. **John Binch**

▲ Heathrow Express 332 008 stands at London Paddington with the 09.10 to Heathrow Airport on 06/08/16. **Alex Dasi-Sutton**

▼ ScotRail Saltire-liveried 334 033 and 334 001 pass Shettleston with the 10.23 Milngavie–Edinburgh Waverley on 11/09/15. **Robert Pritchard**

▲ Brand new Crossrail unit 345 001, in 7-car formation as the first 15 units will be delivered, is seen on the test track at Bombardier Derby on 19/07/16. These units will enter service between London Liverpool Street and Shenfield in May 2017.   **Jonathan Webb**

▼ London Midland-liveried 350 376 leaves Stafford with the 15.04 Liverpool Lime Street–Birmingham New Street on 25/07/15.   **Cliff Beeton**

▲ c2c-liveried 357 321 brings up the rear of the 17.53 London Liverpool Street–Shoeburyness (led by 357 315) at Stratford on 14/08/16.　**Robert Pritchard**

▼ Heathrow Express-liveried 360 205 calls at Southall with the 10.21 Heathrow T4–London Paddington on 06/08/16. This unit normally works the Heathrow T1, 2 & 3–T4 shuttle service.　**Chris Wilson**

▲ Thameslink-liveried 365 505 brings up the rear of the 10.22 London King's Cross–Peterborough, seen leaving King's Cross on 04/07/16.   **Robert Pritchard**

▼ Southeastern blue-liveried 375 704 and 375 707 trail the 15.30 London Charing Cross–Tunbridge Wells (led by white 375 802) at St Johns on 30/08/16.
Tony Christie

▲ Southeastern-liveried 376 010 and 376 028 arrive at Grove Park with the 17.06 Sevenoaks–London Charing Cross on 30/08/16. **Tony Christie**

▼ Southern-liveried 377 467 approaches Horley on 24/08/16. **Gavin Morrison**

▲ London Overground-liveried 378 229 calls at Acton Central with the 15.25 Stratford–Richmond on 15/06/16. **Robert Pritchard**

▼ In white livery with Stansted Express logos, 379 012 and 379 014 pass Silver Street with the diverted 16.15 Stansted Airport–London Liverpool Street on 14/08/16. **Robert Pritchard**

▲ ScotRail Saltire-liveried 380 105 is seen on the Lanark branch with the 09.21 Lanark–Glasgow Central on 27/04/16. **Robin Ralston**

▼ Two of the new Great Western Railway Class 387s, 387 132 and 387 133, pass Acton Mainline with a Heathrow Airport Junction–London Paddington test run on 24/08/16. **Alisdair Anderson**

▲ Virgin Trains-liveried 11-car Pendolino 390 141 passes Stafford on 25/07/15 with the 12.51 Edinburgh Waverley–London Euston. **Cliff Beeton**

▼ Southeastern blue-liveried 395 005 is seen on HS1 between Lenham and Harrietsham with the 17.00 Folkestone Central–London St Pancras on 16/06/16.
Robert Pritchard

▲ Gatwick Express-liveried 442 417 and 442 404 are seen near Salfords with the 15.15 London Victoria–Gatwick Airport on 16/08/16. **Alex Dasi-Sutton**

▼ South West Trains white-liveried 444 023 arrives at Weymouth on 09/07/15 with the 14.05 from London Waterloo. **Stephen Ginn**

▲ Southern-liveried 455 804 arrives at Mitcham Junction with the 13.17 London Victoria–Epsom on 11/04/15. **Robert Pritchard**

▼ South West Trains blue-liveried 458 506 and 458 528 arrive at Twickenham with the 10.08 Staines–London Waterloo on 09/04/16. **Chris Wilson**

▲ Southeastern suburban-liveried 466 024 and 465 242 arrive at Waterloo East with the 11.02 London Charing Cross–Dartford on 12/07/16. **Alex Dasi-Sutton**

▼ Island Line's ex-LUL 483 008 arrives at Sandown with the 16.49 Ryde Pier Head–Shanklin on 13/08/16. **Nick Kelly**

▲ Merseyrail-liveried 508 114 arrives at Bache on 09/08/14 with the 14.30 Liverpool Central–Chester. **Cliff Beeton**

▼ Thameslink-liveried 700 112 arrives at Redhill with the 13.24 Bedford–Three Bridges on 15/08/16. **Alex Dasi-Sutton**

▲ Great Western Railway-liveried IEP 800 004 stands at London Paddington on 30/06/16 having just worked a special from Reading. **Robert Pritchard**

▼ Siemens Velaro e320 Eurostar 4006/05 is seen between Lenham and Harrietsham with the 16.13 Paris–London St Pancras on 16/06/16. **Robert Pritchard**

377463	**SN**	P	*SN*	Bl	73463	78863	78663	73863
377464	**SN**	P	*SN*	Bl	73464	78864	78664	73864
377465	**SN**	P	*SN*	Bl	73465	78865	78665	73865
377466	**SN**	P	*SN*	Bl	73466	78866	78666	73866
377467	**SN**	P	*SN*	Bl	73467	78867	78667	73867
377468	**SN**	P	*SN*	Bl	73468	78868	78668	73868
377469	**SN**	P	*SN*	Bl	73469	78869	78669	73869
377470	**SN**	P	*SN*	Bl	73470	78870	78670	73870
377471	**SN**	P	*SN*	Bl	73471	78871	78671	73871
377472	**SN**	P	*SN*	Bl	73472	78872	78672	73872
377473	**SN**	P	*SN*	Bl	73473	78873	78673	73873
377474	**SN**	P	*SN*	Bl	73474	78874	78674	73874
377475	**SN**	P	*SN*	Bl	73475	78875	78675	73875

Class 377/5. 25kV AC/750V DC. DMCO–MSO–PTSO–DMSO. Dual-voltage Thameslink units. Details as Class 377/2 unless stated.

DMCO. Bombardier Derby 2008–09. 10/48. 43.1t.
MSO. Bombardier Derby 2008–09. –/69 1T. 40.3t.
PTSO. Bombardier Derby 2008–09. –/56 1TD 2W. 40.6 t.
DMSO. Bombardier Derby 2008–09. –/58. 44.9t.

377501	**FB**	P	*TL*	BF	73501	75901	74901	73601
377502	**FB**	P	*TL*	BF	73502	75902	74902	73602
377503	**FU**	P	*TL*	BF	73503	75903	74903	73603
377504	**FB**	P	*TL*	BF	73504	75904	74904	73604
377505	**FB**	P	*TL*	BF	73505	75905	74905	73605
377506	**FB**	P	*TL*	BF	73506	75906	74906	73606
377507	**FB**	P	*TL*	BF	73507	75907	74907	73607
377508	**FB**	P	*TL*	BF	73508	75908	74908	73608
377509	**FU**	P	*TL*	BF	73509	75909	74909	73609
377510	**FB**	P	*TL*	BF	73510	75910	74910	73610
377511	**FB**	P	*TL*	BF	73511	75911	74911	73611
377512	**FB**	P	*TL*	BF	73512	75912	74912	73612
377513	**FB**	P	*TL*	BF	73513	75913	74913	73613
377514	**FU**	P	*TL*	BF	73514	75914	74914	73614
377515	**FU**	P	*TL*	BF	73515	75915	74915	73615
377516	**FU**	P	*TL*	BF	73516	75916	74916	73616
377517	**FU**	P	*TL*	BF	73517	75917	74917	73617
377518	**FU**	P	*TL*	BF	73518	75918	74918	73618
377519	**FU**	P	*TL*	BF	73519	75919	74919	73619
377520	**FU**	P	*TL*	BF	73520	75920	74920	73620
377521	**FU**	P	*TL*	BF	73521	75921	74921	73621
377522	**FU**	P	*TL*	BF	73522	75922	74922	73622
377523	**FU**	P	*TL*	BF	73523	75923	74923	73623

Class 377/6. 750V DC. DMSO–MSO–TSO–MSO–DMSO. Southern 5-car suburban units fitted with Fainsa seating. Technically the same as the 377/5s but using the slightly modified Class 379-style bodyshell.
Seating Layout: 2+2 facing/unidirectional.

DMSO. Bombardier Derby 2012–13. 24/36. 44.7 t.
MSO. Bombardier Derby 2012–13. –/64 1T. 38.8 t.
TSO. Bombardier Derby 2012–13. –/46(+2) 1TD 2W. 37.8 t.
MSO. Bombardier Derby 2012–13. –/66. 38.3 t.
DMSO. Bombardier Derby 2012–13. –/62. 44.7 t.

377601	**SN**	P	*SN*	SU	70101	70201	70301	70401	70501
377602	**SN**	P	*SN*	SU	70102	70202	70302	70402	70502
377603	**SN**	P	*SN*	SU	70103	70203	70303	70403	70503
377604	**SN**	P	*SN*	SU	70104	70204	70304	70404	70504
377605	**SN**	P	*SN*	SU	70105	70205	70305	70405	70505
377606	**SN**	P	*SN*	SU	70106	70206	70306	70406	70506
377607	**SN**	P	*SN*	SU	70107	70207	70307	70407	70507
377608	**SN**	P	*SN*	SU	70108	70208	70308	70408	70508
377609	**SN**	P	*SN*	SU	70109	70209	70309	70409	70509
377610	**SN**	P	*SN*	SU	70110	70210	70310	70410	70510
377611	**SN**	P	*SN*	SU	70111	70211	70311	70411	70511
377612	**SN**	P	*SN*	SU	70112	70212	70312	70412	70512
377613	**SN**	P	*SN*	SU	70113	70213	70313	70413	70513
377614	**SN**	P	*SN*	SU	70114	70214	70314	70414	70514
377615	**SN**	P	*SN*	SU	70115	70215	70315	70415	70515
377616	**SN**	P	*SN*	SU	70116	70216	70316	70416	70516
377617	**SN**	P	*SN*	SU	70117	70217	70317	70417	70517
377618	**SN**	P	*SN*	SU	70118	70218	70318	70418	70518
377619	**SN**	P	*SN*	SU	70119	70219	70319	70419	70519
377620	**SN**	P	*SN*	SU	70120	70220	70320	70420	70520
377621	**SN**	P	*SN*	SU	70121	70221	70321	70421	70521
377622	**SN**	P	*SN*	SU	70122	70222	70322	70422	70522
377623	**SN**	P	*SN*	SU	70123	70223	70323	70423	70523
377624	**SN**	P	*SN*	SU	70124	70224	70324	70424	70524
377625	**SN**	P	*SN*	SU	70125	70225	70325	70425	70525
377626	**SN**	P	*SN*	SU	70126	70226	70326	70426	70526

Class 377/7. 25kV AC/750V DC. DMSO–MSO–TSO–MSO–DMSO. Dual-voltage Southern units, used on both the South Croydon–Milton Keynes cross-London services and on suburban services alongside the 377/6s.

DMSO. Bombardier Derby 2013–14. 24/36. 45.6 t.
MSO. Bombardier Derby 2013–14. –/64 1T. 41.0 t.
PTSO. Bombardier Derby 2013–14. –/46(+2) 1TD 2W. 40.9 t.
MSO. Bombardier Derby 2013–14. –/66. 39.6 t.
DMSO. Bombardier Derby 2013–14. –/62. 45.2 t.

377701	**SN**	P	*SN*	SU	65201	70601	65601	70701	65401
377702	**SN**	P	*SN*	SU	65202	70602	65602	70702	65402
377703	**SN**	P	*SN*	SU	65203	70603	65603	70703	65403
377704	**SN**	P	*SN*	SU	65204	70604	65604	70704	65404
377705	**SN**	P	*SN*	SU	65205	70605	65605	70705	65405
377706	**SN**	P	*SN*	SU	65206	70606	65606	70706	65406
377707	**SN**	P	*SN*	SU	65207	70607	65607	70707	65407
377708	**SN**	P	*SN*	SU	65208	70608	65608	70708	65408

CLASS 378   CAPITALSTAR   BOMBARDIER DERBY

These suburban Electrostars are designated Capitalstars by TfL.

Formation: DMSO–MSO–TSO–MSO–DMSO   or   DMSO–MSO–PTSO–MSO–DMSO.
System: Class 378/1 750 V DC third rail only. Class 378/2 25 kV AC overhead and 750 V DC third rail.
Construction: Welded aluminium alloy underframe, sides and roof with steel ends. All sections bolted together.
Traction Motors: Two Bombardier asynchronous of 200 kW.
Wheel Arrangement: 1A-Bo + 1A-Bo + 2-2 + Bo-1A + Bo-1A.
Braking: Disc & regenerative.   **Dimensions:** 20.46/20.14 x 2.80 m.
Bogies: Bombardier P3-25/T3-25.   **Couplers:** Dellner 12.
Gangways: Within unit + end doors.   **Control System:** IGBT Inverter.
Doors: Sliding.   **Maximum Speed:** 75 mph.
Heating & ventilation: Air conditioning.
Seating Layout: Longitudinal ("tube style") low density.
Multiple Working: Within class and with Classes 375, 376, 377 and 379.

57 extra MSOs (in the 384xx number series) were delivered 2014–15 to make all units up to 5-cars.

Class 378/1. 750 V DC. DMSO–MSO–TSO–MSO–DMSO. Third rail only units used on the East London Line. Provision for retro-fitting as dual voltage.

378 150–154 are fitted with de-icing equipment.

DMSO(A). Bombardier Derby 2009–10. –/36. 43.1 t.
MSO(A). Bombardier Derby 2009–10. –/40. 39.3 t.
TSO. Bombardier Derby 2009–10. –/34(+6) 2W. 34.3t.
MSO(B). Bombardier Derby 2014–15. –/40. 40.2 t.
DMSO(B). Bombardier Derby 2009–10. –/36. 42.7 t.

378 135	L0	QW	*LO*	NG	38035	38235	38335	38435	38135
378 136	L0	QW	*LO*	NG	38036	38236	38336	38436	38136
378 137	L0	QW	*LO*	NG	38037	38237	38337	38437	38137
378 138	L0	QW	*LO*	NG	38038	38238	38338	38438	38138
378 139	L0	QW	*LO*	NG	38039	38239	38339	38439	38139
378 140	L0	QW	*LO*	NG	38040	38240	38340	38440	38140
378 141	L0	QW	*LO*	NG	38041	38241	38341	38441	38141
378 142	L0	QW	*LO*	NG	38042	38242	38342	38442	38142
378 143	L0	QW	*LO*	NG	38043	38243	38343	38443	38143
378 144	L0	QW	*LO*	NG	38044	38244	38344	38444	38144
378 145	L0	QW	*LO*	NG	38045	38245	38345	38445	38145
378 146	L0	QW	*LO*	NG	38046	38246	38346	38446	38146
378 147	L0	QW	*LO*	NG	38047	38247	38347	38447	38147
378 148	L0	QW	*LO*	NG	38048	38248	38348	38448	38148
378 149	L0	QW	*LO*	NG	38049	38249	38349	38449	38149
378 150	L0	QW	*LO*	NG	38050	38250	38350	38450	38150
378 151	L0	QW	*LO*	NG	38051	38251	38351	38451	38151
378 152	L0	QW	*LO*	NG	38052	38252	38352	38452	38152
378 153	L0	QW	*LO*	NG	38053	38253	38353	38453	38153
378 154	L0	QW	*LO*	NG	38054	38254	38354	38454	38154

Class 378/2. 25 kV AC/750 V DC. DMSO–MSO–PTSO–MSO–DMSO. Dual-voltage units mainly used on North London Railway services. 378 201–224 were built as 3-car units 378 001–024 and extended to 4-car units in 2010.

Fitted with tripcocks for operation on the tracks shared with London Underground between Queens Park and Harrow & Wealdstone.

378 216–220 are fitted with de-icing equipment.

DMSO(A). Bombardier Derby 2008–11. –/36. 43.4 t.
MSO(A). Bombardier Derby 2008–11. –/40. 39.6 t.
PTSO. Bombardier Derby 2008–11. –/34(+6) 2W. 39.2 t.
MSO(B). Bombardier Derby 2014–15. –/40. 40.4 t.
DMSO(B). Bombardier Derby 2008–11. –/36. 43.1 t.

378 201	**LO**	QW	*LO*	NG	38001	38201	38301	38401	38101
378 202	**LO**	QW	*LO*	NG	38002	38202	38302	38402	38102
378 203	**LO**	QW	*LO*	NG	38003	38203	38303	38403	38103
378 204	**LO**	QW	*LO*	NG	38004	38204	38304	38404	38104
378 205	**LO**	QW	*LO*	NG	38005	38205	38305	38405	38105
378 206	**LO**	QW	*LO*	NG	38006	38206	38306	38406	38106
378 207	**LO**	QW	*LO*	NG	38007	38207	38307	38407	38107
378 208	**LO**	QW	*LO*	NG	38008	38208	38308	38408	38108
378 209	**LO**	QW	*LO*	NG	38009	38209	38309	38409	38109
378 210	**LO**	QW	*LO*	NG	38010	38210	38310	38410	38110
378 211	**LO**	QW	*LO*	NG	38011	38211	38311	38411	38111
378 212	**LO**	QW	*LO*	NG	38012	38212	38312	38412	38112
378 213	**LO**	QW	*LO*	NG	38013	38213	38313	38413	38113
378 214	**LO**	QW	*LO*	NG	38014	38214	38314	38414	38114
378 215	**LO**	QW	*LO*	NG	38015	38215	38315	38415	38115
378 216	**LO**	QW	*LO*	NG	38016	38216	38316	38416	38116
378 217	**LO**	QW	*LO*	NG	38017	38217	38317	38417	38117
378 218	**LO**	QW	*LO*	NG	38018	38218	38318	38418	38118
378 219	**LO**	QW	*LO*	NG	38019	38219	38319	38419	38119
378 220	**LO**	QW	*LO*	NG	38020	38220	38320	38420	38120
378 221	**LO**	QW	*LO*	NG	38021	38221	38321	38421	38121
378 222	**LO**	QW	*LO*	NG	38022	38222	38322	38422	38122
378 223	**LO**	QW	*LO*	NG	38023	38223	38323	38423	38123
378 224	**LO**	QW	*LO*	NG	38024	38224	38324	38424	38124
378 225	**LO**	QW	*LO*	NG	38025	38225	38325	38425	38125
378 226	**LO**	QW	*LO*	NG	38026	38226	38326	38426	38126
378 227	**LO**	QW	*LO*	NG	38027	38227	38327	38427	38127
378 228	**LO**	QW	*LO*	NG	38028	38228	38328	38428	38128
378 229	**LO**	QW	*LO*	NG	38029	38229	38329	38429	38129
378 230	**LO**	QW	*LO*	NG	38030	38230	38330	38430	38130
378 231	**LO**	QW	*LO*	NG	38031	38231	38331	38431	38131
378 232	**LO**	QW	*LO*	NG	38032	38232	38332	38432	38132
378 233	**LO**	QW	*LO*	NG	38033	38233	38333	38433	38133
378 234	**LO**	QW	*LO*	NG	38034	38234	38334	38434	38134
378 255	**LO**	QW	*LO*	NG	38055	38255	38355	38455	38155
378 256	**LO**	QW	*LO*	NG	38056	38256	38356	38456	38156
378 257	**LO**	QW	*LO*	NG	38057	38257	38357	38457	38157

Names (carried on DMSO(A)):

378204 Professor Sir Peter Hall | 378233   Ian Brown CBE

CLASS 379   ELECTROSTAR   BOMBARDIER DERBY

Express Electrostars used on Liverpool Street–Stansted Airport and Liverpool Street–Cambridge services.

Formation: DMSO–MSO–PTSO–DMCO.
System: 25 kV AC overhead.
Construction: Welded aluminium alloy underframe, sides and roof with steel ends. All sections bolted together.
Traction Motors: Two Bombardier asynchronous of 200 kW.
Wheel Arrangement: 2-Bo + 2-Bo + 2-2 + Bo-2.

Braking: Disc & regenerative.	**Dimensions:** 20.00 x 2.80 m.
Bogies: Bombardier P3-25/T3-25.	**Couplers:** Dellner 12.
Gangways: Throughout.	**Control System:** IGBT Inverter.
Doors: Sliding plug.	**Maximum Speed:** 100 mph.

Heating & ventilation: Air conditioning.
Seating Layout: 1: 2+1 facing. 2: 2+2 facing/unidirectional.
Multiple Working: Within class and with Classes 375, 376, 377 and 378.

DMSO. Bombardier Derby 2010–11. –/60. 42.1 t.
MSO. Bombardier Derby 2010–11. –/62 1T. 38.6 t.
PTSO. Bombardier Derby 2010–11. –/43(+2) 1TD 2W. 40.9 t.
DMCO. Bombardier Derby 2010–11. 20/24. 42.3 t.

379001	**NC**	MQ	*GA*	IL	61201	61701	61901	62101
379002	**NC**	MQ	*GA*	IL	61202	61702	61902	62102
379003	**NC**	MQ	*GA*	IL	61203	61703	61903	62103
379004	**NC**	MQ	*GA*	IL	61204	61704	61904	62104
379005	**NC**	MQ	*GA*	IL	61205	61705	61905	62105
379006	**NC**	MQ	*GA*	IL	61206	61706	61906	62106
379007	**NC**	MQ	*GA*	IL	61207	61707	61907	62107
379008	**NC**	MQ	*GA*	IL	61208	61708	61908	62108
379009	**NC**	MQ	*GA*	IL	61209	61709	61909	62109
379010	**NC**	MQ	*GA*	IL	61210	61710	61910	62110
379011	**NC**	MQ	*GA*	IL	61211	61711	61911	62111
379012	**NC**	MQ	*GA*	IL	61212	61712	61912	62112
379013	**NC**	MQ	*GA*	IL	61213	61713	61913	62113
379014	**NC**	MQ	*GA*	IL	61214	61714	61914	62114
379015	**NC**	MQ	*GA*	IL	61215	61715	61915	62115
379016	**NC**	MQ	*GA*	IL	61216	61716	61916	62116
379017	**NC**	MQ	*GA*	IL	61217	61717	61917	62117
379018	**NC**	MQ	*GA*	IL	61218	61718	61918	62118
379019	**NC**	MQ	*GA*	IL	61219	61719	61919	62119
379020	**NC**	MQ	*GA*	IL	61220	61720	61920	62120
379021	**NC**	MQ	*GA*	IL	61221	61721	61921	62121
379022	**NC**	MQ	*GA*	IL	61222	61722	61922	62122
379023	**NC**	MQ	*GA*	IL	61223	61723	61923	62123
379024	**NC**	MQ	*GA*	IL	61224	61724	61924	62124
379025	**NC**	MQ	*GA*	IL	61225	61725	61925	62125

379026	**NC**	MQ	*GA*	IL	61226	61726	61926	62126
379027	**NC**	MQ	*GA*	IL	61227	61727	61927	62127
379028	**NC**	MQ	*GA*	IL	61228	61728	61928	62128
379029	**NC**	MQ	*GA*	IL	61229	61729	61929	62129
379030	**NC**	MQ	*GA*	IL	61230	61730	61930	62130

Names (carried on end cars):

379005	Stansted Express	379015	City of Cambridge
379011	Ely Cathedral	379025	Go Discover
379012	The West Anglian		

CLASS 380   DESIRO UK   SIEMENS

Used on Strathclyde area services and the Edinburgh–North Berwick route.

Formation: DMSO–PTSO–DMSO or DMSO–PTSO–TSO–DMSO.
System: 25 kV AC overhead.
Construction: Welded aluminium with steel ends.
Traction Motors: Four Siemens ITB2016-0GB02 asynchronous of 250 kW.
Wheel Arrangement: Bo-Bo + 2-2 (+2-2) + Bo-Bo

Braking: Disc & regenerative.	**Dimensions:** 23.78/23.57 x 2.80 m.
Bogies: SGP SF5000.	**Couplers:** Voith.
Gangways: Throughout.	**Control System:** IGBT Inverter.
Doors: Sliding plug.	**Maximum Speed:** 100 mph.
Heating & ventilation: Air conditioning.	**Seating Layout:** 2+2 facing/unidirectional.

Multiple Working: Within class.

DMSO(A). Siemens Krefeld 2009–10. –/70. 45.0 t.
PTSO. Siemens Krefeld 2009–10. –/57(+12) 1TD 2W. 42.7 t.
TSO. Siemens Krefeld 2009–10. –/74 1T. 34.8 t.
DMSO(B). Siemens Krefeld 2009–10. –/64(+5). 44.9 t.

Class 380/0. 3-car units. **Formation:** DMSO–PTSO–DMSO.

380001	**SR**	E	*SR*	GW	38501	38601	38701
380002	**SR**	E	*SR*	GW	38502	38602	38702
380003	**SR**	E	*SR*	GW	38503	38603	38703
380004	**SR**	E	*SR*	GW	38504	38604	38704
380005	**SR**	E	*SR*	GW	38505	38605	38705
380006	**SR**	E	*SR*	GW	38506	38606	38706
380007	**SR**	E	*SR*	GW	38507	38607	38707
380008	**SR**	E	*SR*	GW	38508	38608	38708
380009	**SR**	E	*SR*	GW	38509	38609	38709
380010	**SR**	E	*SR*	GW	38510	38610	38710
380011	**SR**	E	*SR*	GW	38511	38611	38711
380012	**SR**	E	*SR*	GW	38512	38612	38712
380013	**SR**	E	*SR*	GW	38513	38613	38713
380014	**SR**	E	*SR*	GW	38514	38614	38714
380015	**SR**	E	*SR*	GW	38515	38615	38715
380016	**SR**	E	*SR*	GW	38516	38616	38716
380017	**SR**	E	*SR*	GW	38517	38617	38717
380018	**SR**	E	*SR*	GW	38518	38618	38718
380019	**SR**	E	*SR*	GW	38519	38619	38719

380020	**SR**	E	*SR*	GW	38520	38620		38720
380021	**SR**	E	*SR*	GW	38521	38621		38721
380022	**SR**	E	*SR*	GW	38522	38622		38722

Class 380/1. 4-car units. **Formation:** DMSO–PTSO–TSO–DMSO.

380101	**SR**	E	*SR*	GW	38551	38651	38851	38751
380102	**SR**	E	*SR*	GW	38552	38652	38852	38752
380103	**SR**	E	*SR*	GW	38553	38653	38853	38753
380104	**SR**	E	*SR*	GW	38554	38654	38854	38754
380105	**SR**	E	*SR*	GW	38555	38655	38855	38755
380106	**SR**	E	*SR*	GW	38556	38656	38856	38756
380107	**SR**	E	*SR*	GW	38557	38657	38857	38757
380108	**SR**	E	*SR*	GW	38558	38658	38858	38758
380109	**SR**	E	*SR*	GW	38559	38659	38859	38759
380110	**SR**	E	*SR*	GW	38560	38660	38860	38760
380111	**SR**	E	*SR*	GW	38561	38661	38861	38761
380112	**SR**	E	*SR*	GW	38562	38662	38862	38762
380113	**SR**	E	*SR*	GW	38563	38663	38863	38763
380114	**SR**	E	*SR*	GW	38564	38664	38864	38764
380115	**SR**	E	*SR*	GW	38565	38665	38865	38765
380116	**SR**	E	*SR*	GW	38566	38666	38866	38766

CLASS 387   ELECTROSTAR   BOMBARDIER DERBY

The first 29 110 mph Class 387/1s were delivered in 2014–15 for Thameslink. During 2016–17 these will transfer to Great Northern for services from King's Cross to Cambridge/Kings Lynn and Peterborough. The 387/1s were the first units to feature 6-digit vehicle numbers.

A further 27 Class 387/2 units were delivered to Southern for Gatwick Express services in 2016.

Great Western Railway has 45 Class 387/1s on order for delivery 2016–17 for newly electrified routes from London Paddington.

Part of a speculative order by Porterbrook Leasing, c2c is taking six Class 387/3s for 3 years from late 2016. Porterbrook had originally placed an order for 20 speculative units (387301–320), but the other 14 from this order will now form part of the GWR Class 387/1 order.

Formation: DMCO–MSO–PTSO–DMSO.
System: 25 kV AC overhead and 750 V DC third rail.
Construction: Welded aluminium alloy underframe, sides and roof with steel ends. All sections bolted together.
Traction Motors: Two Bombardier asynchronous of 250 kW.
Wheel Arrangement: 2-Bo + 2-Bo + 2-2 + Bo-2.   **Dimensions:** 20.39/20.00 x 2.80 m.
Braking: Disc & regenerative.
Bogies: Bombardier P3-25/T3-25.   **Couplers:** Dellner 12.
Gangways: Throughout.   **Control System:** IGBT Inverter.
Doors: Sliding plug.   **Maximum Speed:** 110 mph.
Heating & ventilation: Air conditioning.
Seating Layout: 2+2 facing/unidirectional.
Multiple Working: Within class and with Class 377.

Class 387/1. Units built for Thameslink but due to transfer to Great Northern 2016–17.

DMCO. Bombardier Derby 2014–15. 10/46. 46.0 t.
MSO. Bombardier Derby 2014–15. –/62 1T. 41.3 t.
PTSO. Bombardier Derby 2014–15. –/45(+2) 1TD 2W. 41.6 t.
DMSO. Bombardier Derby 2014–15. –/60. 45.9 t.

387 101	**TG**	P	*TL*	BI	421101	422101	423101	424101
387 102	**TG**	P	*TL*	BI	421102	422102	423102	424102
387 103	**TG**	P	*TL*	BI	421103	422103	423103	424103
387 104	**TG**	P	*GN*	HE	421104	422104	423104	424104
387 105	**TG**	P	*TL*	BI	421105	422105	423105	424105
387 106	**TG**	P	*GN*	HE	421106	422106	423106	424106
387 107	**TG**	P	*TL*	BI	421107	422107	423107	424107
387 108	**TG**	P	*TL*	BI	421108	422108	423108	424108
387 109	**TG**	P	*GN*	HE	421109	422109	423109	424109
387 110	**TG**	P	*GN*	HE	421110	422110	423110	424110
387 111	**TG**	P	*GN*	HE	421111	422111	423111	424111
387 112	**TG**	P	*GN*	HE	421112	422112	423112	424112
387 113	**TG**	P	*TL*	BI	421113	422113	423113	424113
387 114	**TG**	P	*GN*	HE	421114	422114	423114	424114
387 115	**TG**	P	*TL*	BI	421115	422115	423115	424115
387 116	**TG**	P	*TL*	BI	421116	422116	423116	424116
387 117	**TG**	P	*TL*	BI	421117	422117	423117	424117
387 118	**TG**	P	*TL*	BI	421118	422118	423118	424118
387 119	**TG**	P	*GN*	HE	421119	422119	423119	424119
387 120	**TG**	P	*GN*	HE	421120	422120	423120	424120
387 121	**TG**	P	*TL*	BI	421121	422121	423121	424121
387 122	**TG**	P	*TL*	BI	421122	422122	423122	424122
387 123	**TG**	P	*TL*	BI	421123	422123	423123	424123
387 124	**TG**	P	*TL*	BI	421124	422124	423124	424124
387 125	**TG**	P	*TL*	BI	421125	422125	423125	424125
387 126	**TG**	P	*TL*	BI	421126	422126	423126	424126
387 127	**TG**	P	*TL*	BI	421127	422127	423127	424127
387 128	**TG**	P	*TL*	BI	421128	422128	423128	424128
387 129	**TG**	P	*TL*	BI	421129	422129	423129	424129

Class 387/1. Units currently being delivered to Great Western Railway for services from London Paddington. Units are initially based at North Pole depot for day-to-day servicing, returning to Reading for exams.

DMCO. Bombardier Derby 2016–17. –/56. 46.0 t.
MSO. Bombardier Derby 2016–17. –/62 1T. 41.3 t.
PTSO. Bombardier Derby 2016–17. –/45(+2) 1TD 2W. 41.6 t.
DMSO. Bombardier Derby 2016–17. –/60. 45.9 t.

387 130	**GW**	P	*GW*	RG	421130	422130	423130	424130
387 131	**GW**	P	*GW*	RG	421131	422131	423131	424131
387 132	**GW**	P	*GW*	RG	421132	422132	423132	424132
387 133	**GW**	P	*GW*	RG	421133	422133	423133	424133
387 134	**GW**	P	*GW*	RG	421134	422134	423134	424134
387 135	**GW**	P	*GW*	RG	421135	422135	423135	424135

387 136	**GW**	P	*GW*	RG	421136	422136	423136	424136
387 137	**GW**	P	*GW*	RG	421137	422137	423137	424137
387 138	**GW**	P			421138	422138	423138	424138
387 139	**GW**	P			421139	422139	423139	424139
387 140	**GW**	P			421140	422140	423140	424140
387 141	**GW**	P			421141	422141	423141	424141
387 142	**GW**	P			421142	422142	423142	424142
387 143	**GW**	P			421143	422143	423143	424143
387 144	**GW**	P			421144	422144	423144	424144
387 145	**GW**	P			421145	422145	423145	424145
387 146	**GW**	P			421146	422146	423146	424146
387 147	**GW**	P			421147	422147	423147	424147
387 148	**GW**	P			421148	422148	423148	424148
387 149	**GW**	P			421149	422149	423149	424149
387 150	**GW**	P			421150	422150	423150	424150
387 151	**GW**	P			421151	422151	423151	424151
387 152	**GW**	P			421152	422152	423152	424152
387 153	**GW**	P			421153	422153	423153	424153
387 154	**GW**	P			421154	422154	423154	424154
387 155	**GW**	P			421155	422155	423155	424155
387 156	**GW**	P			421156	422156	423156	424156
387 157	**GW**	P			421157	422157	423157	424157
387 158	**GW**	P			421158	422158	423158	424158
387 159	**GW**	P			421159	422159	423159	424159
387 160	**GW**	P			421160	422160	423160	424160
387 161	**GW**	P			421161	422161	423161	424161
387 162	**GW**	P			421162	422162	423162	424162
387 163	**GW**	P			421163	422163	423163	424163
387 164	**GW**	P			421164	422164	423164	424164
387 165	**GW**	P			421165	422165	423165	424165
387 166	**GW**	P			421166	422166	423166	424166
387 167	**GW**	P			421167	422167	423167	424167
387 168	**GW**	P			421168	422168	423168	424168
387 169	**GW**	P			421169	422169	423169	424169
387 170	**GW**	P			421170	422170	423170	424170
387 171	**GW**	P			421171	422171	423171	424171
387 172	**GW**	P			421172	422172	423172	424172
387 173	**GW**	P			421173	422173	423173	424173
387 174	**GW**	P			421174	422174	423174	424174

Class 387/2. Southern units used on Gatwick Express-branded services on the London Victoria–Gatwick Airport–Brighton route.

DMCO. Bombardier Derby 2015–16. 22/34. 46.0 t.
MSO. Bombardier Derby 2015–16. –/60 1T. 41.3 t.
PTSO. Bombardier Derby 2015–16. –/45(+2) 1TD 2W. 41.6 t.
DMSO. Bombardier Derby 2015–16. –/60. 45.9 t.

387 201	**GX**	P	*SN*	SL	421201	422201	423201	424201
387 202	**GX**	P	*SN*	SL	421202	422202	423202	424202
387 203	**GX**	P	*SN*	SL	421203	422203	423203	424203
387 204	**GX**	P	*SN*	SL	421204	422204	423204	424204

387 205	**GX**	P	*SN*	SL	421205	422205	423205	424205
387 206	**GX**	P	*SN*	SL	421206	422206	423206	424206
387 207	**GX**	P	*SN*	SL	421207	422207	423207	424207
387 208	**GX**	P	*SN*	SL	421208	422208	423208	424208
387 209	**GX**	P	*SN*	SL	421209	422209	423209	424209
387 210	**GX**	P	*SN*	SL	421210	422210	423210	424210
387 211	**GX**	P	*SN*	SL	421211	422211	423211	424211
387 212	**GX**	P	*SN*	SL	421212	422212	423212	424212
387 213	**GX**	P	*SN*	SL	421213	422213	423213	424213
387 214	**GX**	P	*SN*	SL	421214	422214	423214	424214
387 215	**GX**	P	*SN*	SL	421215	422215	423215	424215
387 216	**GX**	P	*SN*	SL	421216	422216	423216	424216
387 217	**GX**	P	*SN*	SL	421217	422217	423217	424217
387 218	**GX**	P	*SN*	SL	421218	422218	423218	424218
387 219	**GX**	P	*SN*	SL	421219	422219	423219	424219
387 220	**GX**	P	*SN*	SL	421220	422220	423220	424220
387 221	**GX**	P	*SN*	SL	421221	422221	423221	424221
387 222	**GX**	P	*SN*	SL	421222	422222	423222	424222
387 223	**GX**	P	*SN*	SL	421223	422223	423223	424223
387 224	**GX**	P	*SN*	SL	421224	422224	423224	424224
387 225	**GX**	P	*SN*	SL	421225	422225	423225	424225
387 226	**GX**	P	*SN*	SL	421226	422226	423226	424226
387 227	**GX**	P	*SN*	SL	421227	422227	423227	424227

Class 387/3. Units on order for c2c, for delivery late 2016. Originally ordered speculatively by Porterbrook Leasing. Full details awaited.

DMCO. Bombardier Derby 2016.
MSO. Bombardier Derby 2016.
PTSO. Bombardier Derby 2016.
DMSO. Bombardier Derby 2016.

387 301	P		421301	422301	423301	424301
387 302	P		421302	422302	423302	424302
387 303	P		421303	422303	423303	424303
387 304	P		421304	422304	423304	424304
387 305	P		421305	422305	423305	424305
387 306	P		421306	422306	423306	424306

CLASS 390   PENDOLINO   ALSTOM

Tilting units used on the West Coast Main Line.

Formations: As listed below.
Traction Motors: Two Alstom ONIX 800 of 425 kW.
Wheel Arrangement: 1A-A1 + 1A-A1 + 2-2 + 1A-A1 (+ 2-2 + 1A-A1) + 2-2 + 1A-A1 + 2-2 + 1A-A1 + 1A-A1.
Dimensions: 24.80/23.90 x 2.73 m.
Bogies: Fiat-SIG.
Gangways: Within unit.
Doors: Sliding plug.
Seating Layout: 1: 2+1 facing/unidirectional, 2: 2+2 facing/unidirectional.

Construction: Welded aluminium alloy.
Braking: Disc, rheostatic & regenerative.
Couplers: Dellner 12.
Control System: IGBT Inverter.
Maximum Speed: 125 mph.
Heating & ventilation: Air conditioning.

Multiple Working: Within class. Can also be controlled from Class 57/3 locos.

Units up to 390034 were delivered as 8-car sets, without the TSO (688xx). During 2004–05 these units were increased to 9-cars.

62 extra vehicles were built 2010–12 to lengthen 31 sets to 11-cars. On renumbering units were renumbered by adding 100 to the set number. Four new complete 11-car units were also delivered. All these extra vehicles were built at Savigliano in Italy (all original Pendolino vehicles were built at Birmingham).

The 9-car units had their MFO(B) converted to an MSO in 2015 to give them a better balance of Standard to First Class seating.

390033 was written off in the Lambrigg accident of February 2007.

Advertising livery: 390 104 – Black Alstom vinyls on Virgin silver livery.

DMRBFO: Alstom Birmingham/Savigliano 2001–05/2010–12. 18/–. 56.3 t.
MFO(A): Alstom Birmingham/Savigliano 2001–05/2010–12. 37/–(+2) 1TD 1W. 52.3 t.
PTFO: Alstom Birmingham/Savigliano 2001–05/2010–12. 44/– 1T. 51.2 t.
MFO(B: 11-car): Alstom Birmingham/Savigliano 2001–05/2010–12. 46/– 1T. 52.3 t.
MSO(C: 9-car): Alstom Birmingham/Savigliano 2001–05/2010–12. –/76 1T. 52.3 t.
(TSO: Alstom Savigliano 2010–12. –/74 1T. 49.2 t.)
(MSO: Alstom Savigliano 2010–12. –/76 1T. 52.2 t.)
TSO: Alstom Birmingham/Savigliano 2001–05/2010–12. –/76 1T. 45.5 t.
MSO(A): Alstom Birmingham/Savigliano 2001–05/2010–12. –/62(+4) 1TD 1W. 52.0 t.
PTSRMB: Alstom Birmingham/Savigliano 2001–05/2010–12. –/48. 53.2 t.
MSO(B): Alstom Birmingham/Savigliano 2001–05/2010–12. –/62(+2) 1TD 1W. 52.5 t.
DMSO: Alstom Birmingham/Savigliano 2001–05/2010–12. –/46 1T. 54.5 t.

Class 390/0. Original build 9-car units.
Formation: DMRFO–MFO–PTFO–MSO–TSO–MSO–PTSRMB–MSO–DMSO.

390001	**VT**	A	*VW* MA	69101	69401	69501	69601	68801	
				69701	69801	69901	69201		
390002	**VT**	A	*VW* MA	69102	69402	69502	69602	68802	
				69702	69802	69902	69202		
390005	**VT**	A	*VW* MA	69105	69405	69505	69605	68805	
				69705	69805	69905	69205		
390006	**VT**	A	*VW* MA	69106	69406	69506	69606	68806	
				69706	69806	69906	69206		
390008	**VT**	A	*VW* MA	69108	69408	69508	69608	68808	
				69708	69808	69908	69208		
390009	**VT**	A	*VW* MA	69109	69409	69509	69609	68809	
				69709	69809	69909	69209		
390010	**VT**	A	*VW* MA	69110	69410	69510	69610	68810	
				69710	69810	69910	69210		
390011	**VT**	A	*VW* MA	69111	69411	69511	69611	68811	
				69711	69811	69911	69211		
390013	**VT**	A	*VW* MA	69113	69413	69513	69613	68813	
				69713	69813	69913	69213		
390016	**VT**	A	*VW* MA	69116	69416	69516	69616	68816	
				69716	69816	69916	69216		

390020	**VT**	A	*VW* MA	69120	69420	69520	69620	68820
				69720	69820	69920	69220	
390039	**VT**	A	*VW* MA	69139	69439	69539	69639	68839
				69739	69839	69939	69239	
390040	**VT**	A	*VW* MA	69140	69440	69540	69640	68840
				69740	69840	69940	69240	
390042	**VT**	A	*VW* MA	69142	69442	69542	69642	68842
				69742	69842	69942	69242	
390043	**VT**	A	*VW* MA	69143	69443	69543	69643	68843
				69743	69843	69943	69243	
390044	**VT**	A	*VW* MA	69144	69444	69544	69644	68844
				69744	69844	69944	69244	
390045	**VT**	A	*VW* MA	69145	69445	69545	69645	68845
				69745	69845	69945	69245	
390046	**VT**	A	*VW* MA	69146	69446	69546	69646	68846
				69746	69846	69946	69246	
390047	**VT**	A	*VW* MA	69147	69447	69547	69647	68847
				69747	69847	69947	69247	
390049	**VT**	A	*VW* MA	69149	69449	69549	69649	68849
				69749	69849	69949	69249	
390050	**VT**	A	*VW* MA	69150	69450	69550	69650	68850
				69750	69850	69950	69250	

Class 390/1. Original build 9-car units later extended to 11-cars, except 390154–157 which were built new (in Italy) as 11-cars.
Formation: DMRFO–MFO–PTFO–MFO–TSO–MSO–TSO–MSO–PTSRMB–MSO–DMSO.

390103	**VT**	A	*VW* MA	69103	69403	69503	69603	65303	68903
				68803	69703	69803	69903	69203	
390104	**AL**	A	*VW* MA	69104	69404	69504	69604	65304	68904
				68804	69704	69804	69904	69204	
390107	**VT**	A	*VW* MA	69107	69407	69507	69607	65307	68907
				68807	69707	69807	69907	69207	
390112	**VT**	A	*VW* MA	69112	69412	69512	69612	65312	68912
				68812	69712	69812	69912	69212	
390114	**VT**	A	*VW* MA	69114	69414	69514	69614	65314	68914
				68814	69714	69814	69914	69214	
390115	**VT**	A	*VW* MA	69115	69415	69515	69615	65315	68915
				68815	69715	69815	69915	69215	
390117	**VT**	A	*VW* MA	69117	69417	69517	69617	65317	68917
				68817	69717	69817	69917	69217	
390118	**VT**	A	*VW* MA	69118	69418	69518	69618	65318	68918
				68818	69718	69818	69918	69218	
390119	**VT**	A	*VW* MA	69119	69419	69519	69619	65319	68919
				68819	69719	69819	69919	69219	
390121	**VT**	A	*VW* MA	69121	69421	69521	69621	65321	68921
				68821	69721	69821	69921	69221	
390122	**VT**	A	*VW* MA	69122	69422	69522	69622	65322	68922
				68822	69722	69822	69922	69222	
390123	**VT**	A	*VW* MA	69123	69423	69523	69623	65323	68923
				68823	69723	69823	69923	69223	

390 124	**VT**	A	*VW* MA	69124	69424	69524	69624	65324	68924
				68824	69724	69824	69924	69224	
390 125	**VT**	A	*VW* MA	69125	69425	69525	69625	65325	68925
				68825	69725	69825	69925	69225	
390 126	**VT**	A	*VW* MA	69126	69426	69526	69626	65326	68926
				68826	69726	69826	69926	69226	
390 127	**VT**	A	*VW* MA	69127	69427	69527	69627	65327	68927
				68827	69727	69827	69927	69227	
390 128	**VT**	A	*VW* MA	69128	69428	69528	69628	65328	68928
				68828	69728	69828	69928	69228	
390 129	**VT**	A	*VW* MA	69129	69429	69529	69629	65329	68929
				68829	69729	69829	69929	69229	
390 130	**VT**	A	*VW* MA	69130	69430	69530	69630	65330	68930
				68830	69730	69830	69930	69230	
390 131	**VT**	A	*VW* MA	69131	69431	69531	69631	65331	68931
				68831	69731	69831	69931	69231	
390 132	**VT**	A	*VW* MA	69132	69432	69532	69632	65332	68932
				68832	69732	69832	69932	69232	
390 134	**VT**	A	*VW* MA	69134	69434	69534	69634	65334	68934
				68834	69734	69834	69934	69234	
390 135	**VT**	A	*VW* MA	69135	69435	69535	69635	65335	68935
				68835	69735	69835	69935	69235	
390 136	**VT**	A	*VW* MA	69136	69436	69536	69636	65336	68936
				68836	69736	69836	69936	69236	
390 137	**VT**	A	*VW* MA	69137	69437	69537	69637	65337	68937
				68837	69737	69837	69937	69237	
390 138	**VT**	A	*VW* MA	69138	69438	69538	69638	65338	68938
				68838	69738	69838	69938	69238	
390 141	**VT**	A	*VW* MA	69141	69441	69541	69641	65341	68941
				68841	69741	69841	69941	69241	
390 148	**VT**	A	*VW* MA	69148	69448	69548	69648	65348	68948
				68848	69748	69848	69948	69248	
390 151	**VT**	A	*VW* MA	69151	69451	69551	69651	65351	68951
				68851	69751	69851	69951	69251	
390 152	**VT**	A	*VW* MA	69152	69452	69552	69652	65352	68952
				68852	69752	69852	69952	69252	
390 153	**VT**	A	*VW* MA	69153	69453	69553	69653	65353	68953
				68853	69753	69853	69953	69253	
390 154	**VT**	A	*VW* MA	69154	69454	69554	69654	65354	68954
				68854	69754	69854	69954	69254	
390 155	**VT**	A	*VW* MA	69155	69455	69555	69655	65355	68955
				68855	69755	69855	69955	69255	
390 156	**VT**	A	*VW* MA	69156	69456	69556	69656	65356	68956
				68856	69756	69856	69956	69256	
390 157	**VT**	A	*VW* MA	69157	69457	69557	69657	65357	68957
				68857	69757	69857	69957	69257	

Names (carried on MFO No. 696xx):

390001	Virgin Pioneer	390118	Virgin Princess
390002	Stephen Sutton	390119	Virgin Warrior
390005	City of Wolverhampton	390121	Virgin Dream
390006	Tate Liverpool	390122	Penny the Pendolino
390009	Virgin King	390123	Virgin Glory
390009	Treaty of Union	390124	Virgin Venturer
390010	The Cumbrian Spirit	390125	Virgin Stagecoach
390011	City of Lichfield	390126	Virgin Enterprise
390013	Virgin Spirit	390127	Virgin Buccaneer
390016	Virgin Champion	390128	City of Preston
390020	Virgin Cavalier	390129	City of Stoke-on-Trent
390039	Virgin Quest	390130	City of Edinburgh
390040	Virgin Radio Star	390131	City of Liverpool
390042	City of Bangor/Dinas Bangor	390132	City of Birmingham
390043	Virgin Explorer	390134	City of Carlisle
390044	Virgin Lionheart	390135	City of Lancaster
390045	101 Squadron	390136	City of Coventry
390046	Virgin Soldiers	390137	Virgin Difference
390047	CLIC Sargent	390138	City of London
390049	Virgin Express	390141	City of Chester
390050	Virgin Invader	390148	Virgin Harrier
390103	Virgin Hero	390151	Virgin Ambassador
390104	Alstom Pendolino	390152	Virgin Knight
390107	Independence Day Resurgence	390153	Mission Accomplished
390112	Virgin Star	390154	Matthew Flinders
390114	City of Manchester	390155	X-MEN Days of Future Past
390115	Virgin Crusader	390156	Stockport 170
390117	Virgin Prince	390157	Chad Varah

CLASS 395   JAVELIN   HITACHI JAPAN

6-car dual-voltage units used on Southeastern High Speed trains from London St Pancras.

Formation: PDTSO–MSO–MSO–MSO–MSO–PDTSO.
Systems: 25 kV AC overhead/750 V DC third rail.
Construction: Aluminium.
Traction Motors: Four Hitachi asynchronous of 210 kW.
Wheel Arrangement: 2-2 + Bo-Bo + Bo-Bo + Bo-Bo + Bo-Bo + 2-2.
Braking: Disc, rheostatic & regenerative.
Dimensions: 20.88/20.0 x 2.81 m.   **Couplers:** Scharfenberg.
Bogies: Hitachi.   **Control System:** IGBT Inverter.
Gangways: Within unit.   **Maximum Speed:** 140 mph.
Doors: Single-leaf sliding.   **Multiple Working:** Within class only.
Heating & ventilation: Air conditioning.
Seating Layout: 2+2 facing/unidirectional (mainly unidirectional).

PDTSO(A): Hitachi Kasado, Japan 2006–09. –/28(+12) 1TD 2W. 46.7 t.
MSO: Hitachi Kasado, Japan 2006–09. –/66. 45.0t–45.7 t.
PDTSO(B): Hitachi Kasado, Japan 2006–09. –/48 1T. 46.7 t.

395001	**SB**	E	*SE*	AD	39011	39012	39013	39014	39015	39016
395002	**SB**	E	*SE*	AD	39021	39022	39023	39024	39025	39026
395003	**SB**	E	*SE*	AD	39031	39032	39033	39034	39035	39036
395004	**SB**	E	*SE*	AD	39041	39042	39043	39044	39045	39046
395005	**SB**	E	*SE*	AD	39051	39052	39053	39054	39055	39056
395006	**SB**	E	*SE*	AD	39061	39062	39063	39064	39065	39066
395007	**SB**	E	*SE*	AD	39071	39072	39073	39074	39075	39076
395008	**SB**	E	*SE*	AD	39081	39082	39083	39084	39085	39086
395009	**SB**	E	*SE*	AD	39091	39092	39093	39094	39095	39096
395010	**SB**	E	*SE*	AD	39101	39102	39103	39104	39105	39106
395011	**SB**	E	*SE*	AD	39111	39112	39113	39114	39115	39116
395012	**SB**	E	*SE*	AD	39121	39122	39123	39124	39125	39126
395013	**SB**	E	*SE*	AD	39131	39132	39133	39134	39135	39136
395014	**SB**	E	*SE*	AD	39141	39142	39143	39144	39145	39146
395015	**SB**	E	*SE*	AD	39151	39152	39153	39154	39155	39156
395016	**SB**	E	*SE*	AD	39161	39162	39163	39164	39165	39166
395017	**SB**	E	*SE*	AD	39171	39172	39173	39174	39175	39176
395018	**SB**	E	*SE*	AD	39181	39182	39183	39184	39185	39186
395019	**SB**	E	*SE*	AD	39191	39192	39193	39194	39195	39196
395020	**SB**	E	*SE*	AD	39201	39202	39203	39204	39205	39206
395021	**SB**	E	*SE*	AD	39211	39212	39213	39214	39215	39216
395022	**SB**	E	*SE*	AD	39221	39222	39223	39224	39225	39226
395023	**SB**	E	*SE*	AD	39231	39232	39233	39234	39235	39236
395024	**SB**	E	*SE*	AD	39241	39242	39243	39244	39245	39246
395025	**SB**	E	*SE*	AD	39251	39252	39253	39254	39255	39256
395026	**SB**	E	*SE*	AD	39261	39262	39263	39264	39265	39266
395027	**SB**	E	*SE*	AD	39271	39272	39273	39274	39275	39276
395028	**SB**	E	*SE*	AD	39281	39282	39283	39284	39285	39286
395029	**SB**	E	*SE*	AD	39291	39292	39293	39294	39295	39296

Names (carried on end cars):

395001	Dame Kelly Holmes	395018	Mo Farah
395002	Sebastian Coe	395019	Jessica Ennis
395003	Sir Steve Redgrave	395020	Jason Kenny
395004	Sir Chris Hoy	395021	Ed Clancy MBE
395005	Dame Tanni Grey-Thompson	395022	Alistair Brownlee
395006	Daley Thompson	395023	Ellie Simmonds
395007	Steve Backley	395024	Jonnie Peacock
395008	Ben Ainslie	395025	Victoria Pendleton
395009	Rebecca Adlington	395026	Marc Woods
395010	Duncan Goodhew	395027	Hannah Cockcroft
395011	Katherine Grainger	395028	Laura Trott
395016	Jamie Staff	395029	David Weir
395017	Dame Sarah Storey		

2. 750 V DC THIRD RAIL EMUs

These classes use the third rail system at 750 V DC (unless stated). Outer couplers are buckeyes on units built before 1982 with bar couplers within the units. Newer units generally have Dellner outer couplers.

CLASS 442   WESSEX EXPRESS   BREL DERBY

Units built for Waterloo–Bournemouth–Weymouth services. Previously used by South West Trains, used by Southern until 2016 when they were mostly replaced by Class 387/2s. From late 2016 Southern is retaining just six units – 442 402/406/408/410/413/419.

Formation: DTSO(A)–TSO–MBC–TSO(W)–DTSO(B).
Construction: Steel.
Traction Motors: Four EE546 of 300 kW recovered from Class 432s.
Wheel Arrangement: 2-2 + 2-2 + Bo-Bo + 2-2 + 2-2.
Braking: Disc.   **Dimensions**: 23.15/23.00 x 2.74 m.
Bogies: Two BREL P7 motor bogies (MBSO). T3 bogies (trailer cars).
Couplers: Buckeye.   **Control System**: 1986-type.
Gangways: Throughout.   **Maximum Speed**: 100 mph.
Doors: Sliding plug.   **Heating & Ventilation**: Air conditioning.
Seating Layout: 1: 2+1 facing, 2: 2+2 mainly unidirectional.
Multiple Working: Within class and Class 33/1 & 73 locos in an emergency.

DTSO(A). Lot No. 31030 Derby 1988–89. –/74. 38.5 t.
TSO. Lot No. 31032 Derby 1988–89. –/76 2T. 37.5 t.
MBC. Lot No. 31034 Derby 1988–89. 24/28. 55.0 t.
TSO(W). Lot No. 31033 Derby 1988–89. –/66(+4) 1TD 1T 2W. 37.8 t.
DTSO(B). Lot No. 31031 Derby 1988–89. –/74. 37.3 t.

442 401	GV	A		TB	77382	71818	62937	71842	77414
442 402	GV	A	SN	SL	77383	71819	62938	71843	77407
442 403	GV	A		ZG	77384	71820	62941	71844	77408
442 404	GV	A		SL	77385	71821	62939	71845	77409
442 405	GV	A		ZG	77386	71822	62944	71846	77410
442 406	GV	A	SN	SL	77389	71823	62942	71847	77411
442 407	GV	A		EP	77388	71824	62943	71848	77412
442 408	GV	A	SN	SL	77387	71825	62945	71849	77413
442 409	GV	A		EP	77390	71826	62946	71850	77406
442 410	GV	A	SN	SL	77391	71827	62948	71851	77415
442 411	GV	A		SL	77392	71828	62940	71858	77422
442 412	GV	A		EP	77393	71829	62947	71853	77417
442 413	GV	A	SN	SL	77394	71830	62949	71854	77418
442 414	GV	A		ZG	77395	71831	62950	71855	77419
442 415	GV	A		EP	77396	71832	62951	71856	77420
442 416	GV	A		EP	77397	71833	62952	71857	77421
442 417	GV	A		TB	77398	71834	62953	71852	77416
442 418	GV	A		EP	77399	71835	62954	71859	77423
442 419	GV	A	SN	SL	77400	71836	62955	71860	77424
442 420	GV	A		EP	77401	71837	62956	71861	77425

442 421	**GV**	A		SL	77402	71838	62957	71862	77426
442 422	**GV**	A		EP	77403	71839	62958	71863	77427
442 423	**GV**	A		ZG	77404	71840	62959	71864	77428
442 424	**GV**	A		ZG	77405	71841	62960	71865	77429

CLASS 444   DESIRO UK   SIEMENS

Express units.

Formation: DMCO–TSO–TSO–TSORMB–DMSO.
Construction: Aluminium.
Traction Motors: 4 Siemens 1TB2016-0GB02 asynchronous of 250 kW.
Wheel Arrangement: Bo-Bo + 2-2 + 2-2 + 2-2 + Bo-Bo.
Braking: Disc, rheostatic & regenerative. **Dimensions:** 23.57 x 2.80 m.
Bogies: SGP SF5000. **Couplers:** Dellner 12.
Gangways: Throughout. **Control System:** IGBT Inverter.
Doors: Single-leaf sliding plug. **Maximum Speed:** 100 mph.
Heating & Ventilation: Air conditioning.
Seating Layout: 1: 2+1 facing/unidirectional, 2: 2+2 facing/unidirectional.
Multiple Working: Within class and with Class 450.

DMSO. Siemens Vienna/Krefeld 2003–04. –/76. 51.3t.
TSO 67101–145. Siemens Vienna/Krefeld 2003–04. –/76 1T. 40.3t.
TSO 67151–195. Siemens Vienna/Krefeld 2003–04. –/76 1T. 36.8t.
TSORMB. Siemens Vienna/Krefeld 2003–04. –/47 1T 1TD 2W. 42.1t.
DMCO. Siemens Vienna/Krefeld 2003–04. 35/24. 51.3t.

444 001	**ST**	A	*SW*	NT	63801	67101	67151	67201	63851
444 002	**ST**	A	*SW*	NT	63802	67102	67152	67202	63852
444 003	**ST**	A	*SW*	NT	63803	67103	67153	67203	63853
444 004	**ST**	A	*SW*	NT	63804	67104	67154	67204	63854
444 005	**ST**	A	*SW*	NT	63805	67105	67155	67205	63855
444 006	**ST**	A	*SW*	NT	63806	67106	67156	67206	63856
444 007	**ST**	A	*SW*	NT	63807	67107	67157	67207	63857
444 008	**ST**	A	*SW*	NT	63808	67108	67158	67208	63858
444 009	**ST**	A	*SW*	NT	63809	67109	67159	67209	63859
444 010	**ST**	A	*SW*	NT	63810	67110	67160	67210	63860
444 011	**ST**	A	*SW*	NT	63811	67111	67161	67211	63861
444 012	**ST**	A	*SW*	NT	63812	67112	67162	67212	63862
444 013	**ST**	A	*SW*	NT	63813	67113	67163	67213	63863
444 014	**ST**	A	*SW*	NT	63814	67114	67164	67214	63864
444 015	**ST**	A	*SW*	NT	63815	67115	67165	67215	63865
444 016	**ST**	A	*SW*	NT	63816	67116	67166	67216	63866
444 017	**ST**	A	*SW*	NT	63817	67117	67167	67217	63867
444 018	**ST**	A	*SW*	NT	63818	67118	67168	67218	63868
444 019	**ST**	A	*SW*	NT	63819	67119	67169	67219	63869
444 020	**ST**	A	*SW*	NT	63820	67120	67170	67220	63870
444 021	**ST**	A	*SW*	NT	63821	67121	67171	67221	63871
444 022	**ST**	A	*SW*	NT	63822	67122	67172	67222	63872
444 023	**ST**	A	*SW*	NT	63823	67123	67173	67223	63873
444 024	**ST**	A	*SW*	NT	63824	67124	67174	67224	63874
444 025	**ST**	A	*SW*	NT	63825	67125	67175	67225	63875

444026	**ST**	A	*SW*	NT	63826 67126 67176 67226 63876
444027	**ST**	A	*SW*	NT	63827 67127 67177 67227 63877
444028	**ST**	A	*SW*	NT	63828 67128 67178 67228 63878
444029	**ST**	A	*SW*	NT	63829 67129 67179 67229 63879
444030	**ST**	A	*SW*	NT	63830 67130 67180 67230 63880
444031	**ST**	A	*SW*	NT	63831 67131 67181 67231 63881
444032	**ST**	A	*SW*	NT	63832 67132 67182 67232 63882
444033	**ST**	A	*SW*	NT	63833 67133 67183 67233 63883
444034	**ST**	A	*SW*	NT	63834 67134 67184 67234 63884
444035	**ST**	A	*SW*	NT	63835 67135 67185 67235 63885
444036	**ST**	A	*SW*	NT	63836 67136 67186 67236 63886
444037	**ST**	A	*SW*	NT	63837 67137 67187 67237 63887
444038	**ST**	A	*SW*	NT	63838 67138 67188 67238 63888
444039	**ST**	A	*SW*	NT	63839 67139 67189 67239 63889
444040	**ST**	A	*SW*	NT	63840 67140 67190 67240 63890
444041	**ST**	A	*SW*	NT	63841 67141 67191 67241 63891
444042	**ST**	A	*SW*	NT	63842 67142 67192 67242 63892
444043	**ST**	A	*SW*	NT	63843 67143 67193 67243 63893
444044	**ST**	A	*SW*	NT	63844 67144 67194 67244 63894
444045	**ST**	A	*SW*	NT	63845 67145 67195 67245 63895

Names (carried on TSORMB):

| 444001 NAOMI HOUSE | 444018 THE FAB 444 |
| 444012 DESTINATION WEYMOUTH | 444038 SOUTH WESTERN RAILWAY |

CLASS 450   DESIRO UK   SIEMENS

Outer suburban units.

Formation: DMSO–TCO–TSO–DMSO (DMSO–TSO–TCO–DMSO 450 111–127).
Construction: Aluminium.
Traction Motors: 4 Siemens 1TB2016-0GB02 asynchronous of 250 kW.
Wheel Arrangement: Bo-Bo + 2-2 + 2-2 + Bo-Bo.
Braking: Disc, rheostatic & regenerative. **Dimensions:** 20.34 x 2.79 m.
Bogies: SGP SF5000. **Couplers:** Dellner 12.
Gangways: Throughout. **Control System:** IGBT Inverter.
Doors: Sliding plug. **Maximum Speed:** 100 mph.
Heating & Ventilation: Air conditioning.
Seating Layout: 1: 2+2 facing/unidirectional, 2: 3+2 facing/unidirectional.
Multiple Working: Within class and with Class 444.

Class 450/0. Standard units.

DMSO(A). Siemens Krefeld/Vienna 2002–06. –/70. 48.0 t.
TCO. Siemens Krefeld/Vienna 2002–06. 24/32(+4) 1T. 35.8 t.
TSO. Siemens Krefeld/Vienna 2002–06. –/61(+9) 1TD 2W. 39.8 t.
DMSO(B). Siemens Krefeld/Vienna 2002–06. –/70. 48.6 t.

450001	**SD**	A	*SW*	NT	63201 64201 68101 63601
450002	**SD**	A	*SW*	NT	63202 64202 68102 63602
450003	**SD**	A	*SW*	NT	63203 64203 68103 63603
450004	**SD**	A	*SW*	NT	63204 64204 68104 63604
450005	**SD**	A	*SW*	NT	63205 64205 68105 63605

450006	**SD**	A	*SW*	NT	63206	64206	68106	63606
450007	**SD**	A	*SW*	NT	63207	64207	68107	63607
450008	**SD**	A	*SW*	NT	63208	64208	68108	63608
450009	**SD**	A	*SW*	NT	63209	64209	68109	63609
450010	**SD**	A	*SW*	NT	63210	64210	68110	63610
450011	**SD**	A	*SW*	NT	63211	64211	68111	63611
450012	**SD**	A	*SW*	NT	63212	64212	68112	63612
450013	**SD**	A	*SW*	NT	63213	64213	68113	63613
450014	**SD**	A	*SW*	NT	63214	64214	68114	63614
450015	**SD**	A	*SW*	NT	63215	64215	68115	63615
450016	**SD**	A	*SW*	NT	63216	64216	68116	63616
450017	**SD**	A	*SW*	NT	63217	64217	68117	63617
450018	**SD**	A	*SW*	NT	63218	64218	68118	63618
450019	**SD**	A	*SW*	NT	63219	64219	68119	63619
450020	**SD**	A	*SW*	NT	63220	64220	68120	63620
450021	**SD**	A	*SW*	NT	63221	64221	68121	63621
450022	**SD**	A	*SW*	NT	63222	64222	68122	63622
450023	**SD**	A	*SW*	NT	63223	64223	68123	63623
450024	**SD**	A	*SW*	NT	63224	64224	68124	63624
450025	**SD**	A	*SW*	NT	63225	64225	68125	63625
450026	**SD**	A	*SW*	NT	63226	64226	68126	63626
450027	**SD**	A	*SW*	NT	63227	64227	68127	63627
450028	**SD**	A	*SW*	NT	63228	64228	68128	63628
450029	**SD**	A	*SW*	NT	63229	64229	68129	63629
450030	**SD**	A	*SW*	NT	63230	64230	68130	63630
450031	**SD**	A	*SW*	NT	63231	64231	68131	63631
450032	**SD**	A	*SW*	NT	63232	64232	68132	63632
450033	**SD**	A	*SW*	NT	63233	64233	68133	63633
450034	**SD**	A	*SW*	NT	63234	64234	68134	63634
450035	**SD**	A	*SW*	NT	63235	64235	68135	63635
450036	**SD**	A	*SW*	NT	63236	64236	68136	63636
450037	**SD**	A	*SW*	NT	63237	64237	68137	63637
450038	**SD**	A	*SW*	NT	63238	64238	68138	63638
450039	**SD**	A	*SW*	NT	63239	64239	68139	63639
450040	**SD**	A	*SW*	NT	63240	64240	68140	63640
450041	**SD**	A	*SW*	NT	63241	64241	68141	63641
450042	**SD**	A	*SW*	NT	63242	64242	68142	63642
450071	**SD**	A	*SW*	NT	63271	64271	68171	63671
450072	**SD**	A	*SW*	NT	63272	64272	68172	63672
450073	**SD**	A	*SW*	NT	63273	64273	68173	63673
450074	**SD**	A	*SW*	NT	63274	64274	68174	63674
450075	**SD**	A	*SW*	NT	63275	64275	68175	63675
450076	**SD**	A	*SW*	NT	63276	64276	68176	63676
450077	**SD**	A	*SW*	NT	63277	64277	68177	63677
450078	**SD**	A	*SW*	NT	63278	64278	68178	63678
450079	**SD**	A	*SW*	NT	63279	64279	68179	63679
450080	**SD**	A	*SW*	NT	63280	64280	68180	63680
450081	**SD**	A	*SW*	NT	63281	64281	68181	63681
450082	**SD**	A	*SW*	NT	63282	64282	68182	63682
450083	**SD**	A	*SW*	NT	63283	64283	68183	63683
450084	**SD**	A	*SW*	NT	63284	64284	68184	63684

450 085	**SD**	A	*SW*	NT	63285	64285	68185	63685
450 086	**SD**	A	*SW*	NT	63286	64286	68186	63686
450 087	**SD**	A	*SW*	NT	63287	64287	68187	63687
450 088	**SD**	A	*SW*	NT	63288	64288	68188	63688
450 089	**SD**	A	*SW*	NT	63289	64289	68189	63689
450 090	**SD**	A	*SW*	NT	63290	64290	68190	63690
450 091	**SD**	A	*SW*	NT	63291	64291	68191	63691
450 092	**SD**	A	*SW*	NT	63292	64292	68192	63692
450 093	**SD**	A	*SW*	NT	63293	64293	68193	63693
450 094	**SD**	A	*SW*	NT	63294	64294	68194	63694
450 095	**SD**	A	*SW*	NT	63295	64295	68195	63695
450 096	**SD**	A	*SW*	NT	63296	64296	68196	63696
450 097	**SD**	A	*SW*	NT	63297	64297	68197	63697
450 098	**SD**	A	*SW*	NT	63298	64298	68198	63698
450 099	**SD**	A	*SW*	NT	63299	64299	68199	63699
450 100	**SD**	A	*SW*	NT	63300	64300	68200	63700
450 101	**SD**	A	*SW*	NT	63701	66851	66801	63751
450 102	**SD**	A	*SW*	NT	63702	66852	66802	63752
450 103	**SD**	A	*SW*	NT	63703	66853	66803	63753
450 104	**SD**	A	*SW*	NT	63704	66854	66804	63754
450 105	**SD**	A	*SW*	NT	63705	66855	66805	63755
450 106	**SD**	A	*SW*	NT	63706	66856	66806	63756
450 107	**SD**	A	*SW*	NT	63707	66857	66807	63757
450 108	**SD**	A	*SW*	NT	63708	66858	66808	63758
450 109	**SD**	A	*SW*	NT	63709	66859	66809	63759
450 110	**SD**	A	*SW*	NT	63710	66860	66810	63760
450 111	**SD**	A	*SW*	NT	63901	66921	66901	63921
450 112	**SD**	A	*SW*	NT	63902	66922	66902	63922
450 113	**SD**	A	*SW*	NT	63903	66923	66903	63923
450 114	**SD**	A	*SW*	NT	63904	66924	66904	63924
450 115	**SD**	A	*SW*	NT	63905	66925	66905	63925
450 116	**SD**	A	*SW*	NT	63906	66926	66906	63926
450 117	**SD**	A	*SW*	NT	63907	66927	66907	63927
450 118	**SD**	A	*SW*	NT	63908	66928	66908	63928
450 119	**SD**	A	*SW*	NT	63909	66929	66909	63929
450 120	**SD**	A	*SW*	NT	63910	66930	66910	63930
450 121	**SD**	A	*SW*	NT	63911	66931	66911	63931
450 122	**SD**	A	*SW*	NT	63912	66932	66912	63932
450 123	**SD**	A	*SW*	NT	63913	66933	66913	63933
450 124	**SD**	A	*SW*	NT	63914	66934	66914	63934
450 125	**SD**	A	*SW*	NT	63915	66935	66915	63935
450 126	**SD**	A	*SW*	NT	63916	66936	66916	63936
450 127	**SD**	A	*SW*	NT	63917	66937	66917	63937

Names (carried on DMSO(B)):

450 015 DESIRO
450 042 TRELOAR COLLEGE

450 114 FAIRBRIDGE investing in the future

Class 450/5. 28 units converted 2007–08 with First Class removed and a modified seating layout with more standing room (some Standard Class seats were taken out). First Class was refitted in 2013 but the removed Standard Class seats were not refitted so the units have kept their 450 5xx series numbers.

DMSO(A). Siemens Krefeld/Vienna 2002–04. –/64. 48.0 t.
TCO. Siemens Krefeld/Vienna 2002–04. 24/30(+4) 1T. 35.5 t.
TSO. Siemens Krefeld/Vienna 2002–04. –/56(+9) 1TD 2W. 39.8 t.
DMSO(B). Siemens Krefeld/Vienna 2002–04. –/64. 48.6 t.

450543	(450043)	**SD**	A	*SW*	NT	63243	64243	68143	63643
450544	(450044)	**SD**	A	*SW*	NT	63244	64244	68144	63644
450545	(450045)	**SD**	A	*SW*	NT	63245	64245	68145	63645
450546	(450046)	**SD**	A	*SW*	NT	63246	64246	68146	63646
450547	(450047)	**SD**	A	*SW*	NT	63247	64247	68147	63647
450548	(450048)	**SD**	A	*SW*	NT	63248	64248	68148	63648
450549	(450049)	**SD**	A	*SW*	NT	63249	64249	68149	63649
450550	(450050)	**SD**	A	*SW*	NT	63250	64250	68150	63650
450551	(450051)	**SD**	A	*SW*	NT	63251	64251	68151	63651
450552	(450052)	**SD**	A	*SW*	NT	63252	64252	68152	63652
450553	(450053)	**SD**	A	*SW*	NT	63253	64253	68153	63653
450554	(450054)	**SD**	A	*SW*	NT	63254	64254	68154	63654
450555	(450055)	**SD**	A	*SW*	NT	63255	64255	68155	63655
450556	(450056)	**SD**	A	*SW*	NT	63256	64256	68156	63656
450557	(450057)	**SD**	A	*SW*	NT	63257	64257	68157	63657
450558	(450058)	**SD**	A	*SW*	NT	63258	64258	68158	63658
450559	(450059)	**SD**	A	*SW*	NT	63259	64259	68159	63659
450560	(450060)	**SD**	A	*SW*	NT	63260	64260	68160	63660
450561	(450061)	**SD**	A	*SW*	NT	63261	64261	68161	63661
450562	(450062)	**SD**	A	*SW*	NT	63262	64262	68162	63662
450563	(450063)	**SD**	A	*SW*	NT	63263	64263	68163	63663
450564	(450064)	**SD**	A	*SW*	NT	63264	64264	68164	63664
450565	(450065)	**SD**	A	*SW*	NT	63265	64265	68165	63665
450566	(450066)	**SD**	A	*SW*	NT	63266	64266	68166	63666
450567	(450067)	**SD**	A	*SW*	NT	63267	64267	68167	63667
450568	(450068)	**SD**	A	*SW*	NT	63268	64268	68168	63668
450569	(450069)	**SD**	A	*SW*	NT	63269	64269	68169	63669
450570	(450070)	**SD**	A	*SW*	NT	63270	64270	68170	63670

CLASS 455   BREL YORK

Inner suburban units. During 2016–17 the South West Trains fleet of 91 units are being fitted with new AC traction motors by Vossloh Kiepe.

Formation: DTSO–MSO–TSO–DTSO.
Construction: Steel. Class 455/7 TSO have a steel underframe and an aluminium alloy body & roof.
Traction Motors: Four GEC507-20J of 185 kW, some recovered from Class 405s (* Four TSA010163 AC motors of 240 kW).
Wheel Arrangement: 2-2 + Bo-Bo + 2-2 + 2-2.
Braking: Disc (* and regenerative).   **Dimensions:** 19.92/19.83 x 2.82 m.

Bogies: P7 (motor) and T3 (455/8 & 455/9) BX1 (455/7) trailer.
Gangways: Within unit + end doors (sealed on Southern units).
Couplers: Tightlock.   **Maximum Speed:** 75 mph.
Control System: 1982-type, camshaft (* IGBT Inverter).
Doors: Sliding.   **Heating & Ventilation:** Various.
Seating Layout: All units refurbished. SWT units: 2+2 high-back unidirectional/
facing seating. Southern units: 3+2 high back mainly facing seating.
Multiple Working: Within class and with Class 456.

Class 455/7. South West Trains units. Second series with TSOs originally in
Class 508s. Pressure heating & ventilation.

DTSO. Lot No. 30976 1984–85. –/50(+4) 1W. 30.8t.
MSO. Lot No. 30975 1984–85. –/68. 45.7t.
TSO. Lot No. 30944 1979–80. –/68. 26.1t.

5701		**SS**	P	*SW*	WD	77727	62783	71545	77728
5702		**SS**	P	*SW*	WD	77729	62784	71547	77730
5703		**SS**	P	*SW*	WD	77731	62785	71540	77732
5704		**SS**	P	*SW*	WD	77733	62786	71548	77734
5705	*	**SS**	P	*SW*	WD	77735	62787	71565	77736
5706		**SS**	P	*SW*	WD	77737	62788	71534	77738
5707	*	**SS**	P	*SW*	WD	77739	62789	71536	77740
5708		**SS**	P	*SW*	WD	77741	62790	71560	77742
5709	*	**SS**	P	*SW*	WD	77743	62791	71532	77744
5710	*	**SS**	P	*SW*	WD	77745	62792	71566	77746
5711	*	**SS**	P	*SW*	WD	77747	62793	71542	77748
5712		**SS**	P	*SW*	WD	77749	62794	71546	77750
5713	*	**SS**	P	*SW*	WD	77751	62795	71567	77752
5714	*	**SS**	P	*SW*	WD	77753	62796	71539	77754
5715	*	**SS**	P	*SW*	WD	77755	62797	71535	77756
5716	*	**SS**	P	*SW*	WD	77757	62798	71564	77758
5717		**SS**	P	*SW*	WD	77759	62799	71528	77760
5718		**SS**	P	*SW*	WD	77761	62800	71557	77762
5719	*	**SS**	P	*SW*	WD	77763	62801	71558	77764
5720	*	**SS**	P	*SW*	WD	77765	62802	71568	77766
5721	*	**SS**	P	*SW*	WD	77767	62803	71553	77768
5722		**SS**	P	*SW*	WD	77769	62804	71533	77770
5723		**SS**	P	*SW*	WD	77771	62805	71526	77772
5724		**SS**	P	*SW*	WD	77773	62806	71561	77774
5725	*	**SS**	P	*SW*	WD	77775	62807	71541	77776
5726	*	**SS**	P	*SW*	WD	77777	62808	71556	77778
5727		**SS**	P	*SW*	WD	77779	62809	71562	77780
5728		**SS**	P	*SW*	WD	77781	62810	71527	77782
5729		**SS**	P	*SW*	WD	77783	62811	71550	77784
5730		**SS**	P	*SW*	WD	77785	62812	71551	77786
5731	*	**SS**	P	*SW*	WD	77787	62813	71555	77788
5732	*	**SS**	P	*SW*	WD	77789	62814	71552	77790
5733	*	**SS**	P	*SW*	WD	77791	62815	71549	77792
5734		**SS**	P	*SW*	WD	77793	62816	71531	77794
5735		**SS**	P	*SW*	WD	77795	62817	71563	77796
5736		**SS**	P	*SW*	WD	77797	62818	71554	77798

5737		**SS**	P	*SW*	WD	77799	62819	71544	77800
5738	*	**SS**	P	*SW*	WD	77801	62820	71529	77802
5739		**SS**	P	*SW*	WD	77803	62821	71537	77804
5740		**SS**	P	*SW*	WD	77805	62822	71530	77806
5741	*	**SS**	P	*SW*	WD	77807	62823	71559	77808
5742		**SS**	P	*SW*	WD	77809	62824	71543	77810
5750		**SS**	P	*SW*	WD	77811	62825	71538	77812

Class 455/8. Southern units. First series. Pressure heating & ventilation. Fitted with in-cab air conditioning systems meaning that the end door has been sealed.

DTSO. Lot No. 30972 York 1982–84. –/74. 33.6 t.
MSO. Lot No. 30973 York 1982–84. –/84. 45.6 t.
TSO. Lot No. 30974 York 1982–84. –/75(+3) 2W. 34.0 t.

455 801	**SN**	E	*SN*	SL	77627	62709	71657	77580
455 802	**SN**	E	*SN*	SL	77581	62710	71664	77582
455 803	**SN**	E	*SN*	SL	77583	62711	71639	77584
455 804	**SN**	E	*SN*	SL	77585	62712	71640	77586
455 805	**SN**	E	*SN*	SL	77587	62713	71641	77588
455 806	**SN**	E	*SN*	SL	77589	62714	71642	77590
455 807	**SN**	E	*SN*	SL	77591	62715	71643	77592
455 808	**SN**	E	*SN*	SL	77637	62716	71644	77594
455 809	**SN**	E	*SN*	SL	77623	62717	71648	77602
455 810	**SN**	E	*SN*	SL	77597	62718	71646	77598
455 811	**SN**	E	*SN*	SL	77599	62719	71647	77600
455 812	**SN**	E	*SN*	SL	77595	62720	71645	77626
455 813	**SN**	E	*SN*	SL	77603	62721	71649	77604
455 814	**SN**	E	*SN*	SL	77605	62722	71650	77606
455 815	**SN**	E	*SN*	SL	77607	62723	71651	77608
455 816	**SN**	E	*SN*	SL	77609	62724	71652	77633
455 817	**SN**	E	*SN*	SL	77611	62725	71653	77612
455 818	**SN**	E	*SN*	SL	77613	62726	71654	77632
455 819	**SN**	E	*SN*	SL	77615	62727	71637	77616
455 820	**SN**	E	*SN*	SL	77617	62728	71656	77618
455 821	**SN**	E	*SN*	SL	77619	62729	71655	77620
455 822	**SN**	E	*SN*	SL	77621	62730	71658	77622
455 823	**SN**	E	*SN*	SL	77601	62731	71659	77596
455 824	**SN**	E	*SN*	SL	77593	62732	71660	77624
455 825	**SN**	E	*SN*	SL	77579	62733	71661	77628
455 826	**SN**	E	*SN*	SL	77630	62734	71662	77629
455 827	**SN**	E	*SN*	SL	77610	62735	71663	77614
455 828	**SN**	E	*SN*	SL	77631	62736	71638	77634
455 829	**SN**	E	*SN*	SL	77635	62737	71665	77636
455 830	**SN**	E	*SN*	SL	77625	62743	71666	77638
455 831	**SN**	E	*SN*	SL	77639	62739	71667	77640
455 832	**SN**	E	*SN*	SL	77641	62740	71668	77642
455 833	**SN**	E	*SN*	SL	77643	62741	71669	77644
455 834	**SN**	E	*SN*	SL	77645	62742	71670	77646
455 835	**SN**	E	*SN*	SL	77647	62738	71671	77648
455 836	**SN**	E	*SN*	SL	77649	62744	71672	77650

455837	**SN**	E	*SN*	SL	77651	62745	71673	77652
455838	**SN**	E	*SN*	SL	77653	62746	71674	77654
455839	**SN**	E	*SN*	SL	77655	62747	71675	77656
455840	**SN**	E	*SN*	SL	77657	62748	71676	77658
455841	**SN**	E	*SN*	SL	77659	62749	71677	77660
455842	**SN**	E	*SN*	SL	77661	62750	71678	77662
455843	**SN**	E	*SN*	SL	77663	62751	71679	77664
455844	**SN**	E	*SN*	SL	77665	62752	71680	77666
455845	**SN**	E	*SN*	SL	77667	62753	71681	77668
455846	**SN**	E	*SN*	SL	77669	62754	71682	77670

Class 455/8. South West Trains units. First series. Pressure heating & ventilation.

DTSO. Lot No. 30972 York 1982–84. –50(+4) 1W. 29.5 t.
MSO. Lot No. 30973 York 1982–84. –/68. 45.6 t.
TSO. Lot No. 30974 York 1982–84. –/68. 27.1 t.

5847		**SS**	P	*SW*	WD	77671	62755	71683	77672
5848		**SS**	P	*SW*	WD	77673	62756	71684	77674
5849		**SS**	P	*SW*	WD	77675	62757	71685	77676
5850		**SS**	P	*SW*	WD	77677	62758	71686	77678
5851		**SS**	P	*SW*	WD	77679	62759	71687	77680
5852		**SS**	P	*SW*	WD	77681	62760	71688	77682
5853		**SS**	P	*SW*	WD	77683	62761	71689	77684
5854		**SS**	P	*SW*	WD	77685	62762	71690	77686
5855		**SS**	P	*SW*	WD	77687	62763	71691	77688
5856		**SS**	P	*SW*	WD	77689	62764	71692	77690
5857		**SS**	P	*SW*	WD	77691	62765	71693	77692
5858		**SS**	P	*SW*	WD	77693	62766	71694	77694
5859		**SS**	P	*SW*	WD	77695	62767	71695	77696
5860		**SS**	P	*SW*	WD	77697	62768	71696	77698
5861		**SS**	P	*SW*	WD	77699	62769	71697	77700
5862		**SS**	P	*SW*	WD	77701	62770	71698	77702
5863		**SS**	P	*SW*	WD	77703	62771	71699	77704
5864		**SS**	P	*SW*	WD	77705	62772	71700	77706
5865		**SS**	P	*SW*	WD	77707	62773	71701	77708
5866		**SS**	P	*SW*	WD	77709	62774	71702	77710
5867		**SS**	P	*SW*	WD	77711	62775	71703	77712
5868		**SS**	P	*SW*	WD	77713	62776	71704	77714
5869		**SS**	P	*SW*	WD	77715	62777	71705	77716
5870	*	**SS**	P	*SW*	WD	77717	62778	71706	77718
5871		**SS**	P	*SW*	WD	77719	62779	71707	77720
5872		**SS**	P	*SW*	WD	77721	62780	71708	77722
5873		**SS**	P	*SW*	WD	77723	62781	71709	77724
5874		**SS**	P	*SW*	WD	77725	62782	71710	77726

Class 455/9. South West Trains units. Third series. Convection heating.
Dimensions: 19.96/20.18 x 2.82 m.

67301 and 67400 were converted from Class 210 DEMU vehicles to replace accident damaged cars.

DTSO. Lot No. 30991 York 1985. –/50(+4) 1W. 30.7 t.
MSO. Lot No. 30992 York 1985. –/68. 46.3 t.

MSO 67301. Lot No. 30932 Derby 1981. –/68.   t.
TSO. Lot No. 30993 York 1985. –/68. 28.3 t.
TSO 67400. Lot No. 30932 Derby 1981. –/68. 26.5 t.

5901		**SS**	P	*SW*	WD	77813	62826	71714	77814
5902		**SS**	P	*SW*	WD	77815	62827	71715	77816
5903		**SS**	P	*SW*	WD	77817	62828	71716	77818
5904	*	**SS**	P	*SW*	WD	77819	62829	71717	77820
5905		**SS**	P	*SW*	WD	77821	62830	71725	77822
5906		**SS**	P	*SW*	WD	77823	62831	71719	77824
5907		**SS**	P	*SW*	WD	77825	62832	71720	77826
5908		**SS**	P	*SW*	WD	77827	62833	71721	77828
5909		**SS**	P	*SW*	WD	77829	62834	71722	77830
5910		**SS**	P	*SW*	WD	77831	62835	71723	77832
5911		**SS**	P	*SW*	WD	77833	62836	71724	77834
5912		**SS**	P	*SW*	WD	77835	62837	67400	77836
5913		**SS**	P	*SW*	WD	77837	67301	71726	77838
5914		**SS**	P	*SW*	WD	77839	62839	71727	77840
5915		**SS**	P	*SW*	WD	77841	62840	71728	77842
5916	*	**SS**	P	*SW*	WD	77843	62841	71729	77844
5917		**SS**	P	*SW*	WD	77845	62842	71730	77846
5918		**SS**	P	*SW*	WD	77847	62843	71732	77848
5919		**SS**	P	*SW*	WD	77849	62844	71718	77850
5920		**SS**	P	*SW*	WD	77851	62845	71733	77852

CLASS 456   BREL YORK

Inner suburban units previously operated by Southern, but operated by South West Trains (following refurbishment) from 2014–15.

Formation: DMSO–DTSO.
Construction: Steel underframe, aluminium alloy body & roof.
Traction Motors: Two GEC507-21J of 185 kW, some recovered from Class 405s.
Wheel Arrangement: 2-Bo + 2-2.   **Dimensions:** 20.61 x 2.82 m.
Braking: Disc.   **Couplers:** Tightlock.
Bogies: P7 (motor) and T3 (trailer).   **Control System:** GTO Chopper.
Gangways: Within unit.   **Maximum Speed:** 75 mph.
Doors: Sliding.
Seating Layout: 2+2 facing/unidirectional.
Heating & Ventilation: Convection heating.
Multiple Working: Within class and with Class 455.

DMSO. Lot No. 31073 1990–91. –/59. 43.3 t.
DTSO. Lot No. 31074 1990–91. –/54(+5). 32.3 t.

456 001	**SS**	P	*SW*	WD	64735	78250
456 002	**SS**	P	*SW*	WD	64736	78251
456 003	**SS**	P	*SW*	WD	64737	78252
456 004	**SS**	P	*SW*	WD	64738	78253
456 005	**SS**	P	*SW*	WD	64739	78254
456 006	**SS**	P	*SW*	WD	64740	78255
456 007	**SS**	P	*SW*	WD	64741	78256

456008	**SS**	P	*SW*	WD	64742	78257
456009	**SS**	P	*SW*	WD	64743	78258
456010	**SS**	P	*SW*	WD	64744	78259
456011	**SS**	P	*SW*	WD	64745	78260
456012	**SS**	P	*SW*	WD	64746	78261
456013	**SS**	P	*SW*	WD	64747	78262
456014	**SS**	P	*SW*	WD	64748	78263
456015	**SS**	P	*SW*	WD	64749	78264
456016	**SS**	P	*SW*	WD	64750	78265
456017	**SS**	P	*SW*	WD	64751	78266
456018	**SS**	P	*SW*	WD	64752	78267
456019	**SS**	P	*SW*	WD	64753	78268
456020	**SS**	P	*SW*	WD	64754	78269
456021	**SS**	P	*SW*	WD	64755	78270
456022	**SS**	P	*SW*	WD	64756	78271
456023	**SS**	P	*SW*	WD	64757	78272
456024	**SS**	P	*SW*	WD	64758	78273

CLASS 458   JUNIPER   ALSTOM BIRMINGHAM

Outer suburban units. Between 2013 and early 2016 the fleet of 30 4-car Class 458 units and the former Gatwick Express fleet of eight 8-car Class 460 units was combined to form a fleet of 36 5-car Standard Class only Class 458/5s. The work was carried out at Wabtec Doncaster and Brush Loughborough. Former Class 460 driving cars 67901/903/907/908 were not included in this programme and have been scrapped.

After lengthening each unit was renumbered into the 458 5xx series. All individual vehicles retained their original numbers.

Formation: DMSO–TSO*–TSO–MSO–DMSO (* ex-Class 460 in 458 501–530).
Construction: Steel.   **Dimensions:** 21.16 or 21.06 x 2.80 m.
Traction Motors: Two Alstom ONIX 800 asynchronous of 270 kW.
Wheel Arrangement: 2-Bo + 2-2 + 2-2 + Bo-2 + Bo-2.
Braking: Disc & regenerative.   **Control System:** IGBT Inverter.
Bogies: ACR.   **Doors:** Sliding plug.
Gangways: Throughout.
Couplers: Voith 136.
Maximum Speed: 75 mph.
Heating & Ventilation: Air conditioning. **Multiple Working:** Within class.
Seating Layout: 2+2 facing/unidirectional.

DMSO(A). Alstom 1998–2000. –/60. 45.7 t.
TSO: Alstom 1998–99. 458 501–530 –/56; 458 531–536 –/52 1T. 34.4 t.
TSO. Alstom 1998–2000. –/42 1TD 2W. 34.1 t.
MSO. Alstom 1998–2000. 458 501–530 –/56 1T; 458 531–536 –/56. 40.1 t.
DMSO(B). Alstom 1998–2000. –/60. 44.9 t.

458501	**SD**	P	*SW*	WD	67601 74431 74001 74101 67701
458502	**SD**	P	*SW*	WD	67602 74421 74002 74102 67702
458503	**SD**	P	*SW*	WD	67603 74441 74003 74103 67703
458504	**SD**	P	*SW*	WD	67604 74451 74004 74104 67704

458505	**SD**	P	*SW*	WD	67605	74425	74005	74105	67705
458506	**SD**	P	*SW*	WD	67606	74436	74006	74106	67706
458507	**SD**	P	*SW*	WD	67607	74428	74007	74107	67707
458508	**SD**	P	*SW*	WD	67608	74433	74008	74108	67708
458509	**SD**	P	*SW*	WD	67609	74452	74009	74109	67709
458510	**SD**	P	*SW*	WD	67610	74405	74010	74110	67710
458511	**SD**	P	*SW*	WD	67611	74435	74011	74111	67711
458512	**SD**	P	*SW*	WD	67612	74427	74012	74112	67712
458513	**SD**	P	*SW*	WD	67613	74437	74013	74113	67713
458514	**SD**	P	*SW*	WD	67614	74407	74014	74114	67714
458515	**SD**	P	*SW*	WD	67615	74404	74015	74115	67715
458516	**SD**	P	*SW*	WD	67616	74406	74016	74116	67716
458517	**SD**	P	*SW*	WD	67617	74426	74017	74117	67717
458518	**SD**	P	*SW*	WD	67618	74432	74018	74118	67718
458519	**SD**	P	*SW*	WD	67619	74403	74019	74119	67719
458520	**SD**	P	*SW*	WD	67620	74401	74020	74120	67720
458521	**SD**	P	*SW*	WD	67621	74438	74021	74121	67721
458522	**SD**	P	*SW*	WD	67622	74424	74022	74122	67722
458523	**SD**	P	*SW*	WD	67623	74434	74023	74123	67723
458524	**SD**	P	*SW*	WD	67624	74402	74024	74124	67724
458525	**SD**	P	*SW*	WD	67625	74422	74025	74125	67725
458526	**SD**	P	*SW*	WD	67626	74442	74026	74126	67726
458527	**SD**	P	*SW*	WD	67627	74412	74027	74127	67727
458528	**SD**	P	*SW*	WD	67628	74408	74028	74128	67728
458529	**SD**	P	*SW*	WD	67629	74423	74029	74129	67729
458530	**SD**	P	*SW*	WD	67630	74411	74030	74130	67730

The following units were converted entirely from Class 460s.

458531	**SD**	P	*SW*	WD	67913	74418	74446	74458	67912
458532	**SD**	P	*SW*	WD	67904	74417	74447	74457	67905
458533	**SD**	P	*SW*	WD	67917	74413	74443	74453	67916
458534	**SD**	P	*SW*	WD	67914	74414	74444	74454	67918
458535	**SD**	P	*SW*	WD	67915	74415	74445	74455	67911
458536	**SD**	P	*SW*	WD	67906	74416	74448	74456	67902

CLASS 465   NETWORKER

Inner/outer suburban units.

Formation: DMSO–TSO–TSO–DMSO.
Construction: Welded aluminium alloy.
Traction Motors: Hitachi asynchronous of 280 kW (Classes 465/0 and 465/1) or GEC-Alsthom G352BY (Classes 465/2 and 465/9).
Wheel Arrangement: Bo-Bo + 2-2 + 2-2 + Bo-Bo.
Braking: Disc & rheostatic and regenerative (Classes 465/0 and 465/1 only).
Bogies: BREL P3/T3 (465/0 and 465/1), SRP BP62/BT52 (465/2 and 465/9).
Dimensions: 20.89/20.06 x 2.81 m.
Control System: IGBT Inverter (465/0 and 465/1) or 1992-type GTO Inverter.
Gangways: Within unit.   **Couplers:** Tightlock.
Doors: Sliding plug.   **Maximum Speed:** 75 mph.
Seating Layout: 3+2 facing/unidirectional.

Multiple Working: Within class and with Class 466.

64759–808. DMSO(A). Lot No. 31100 BREL York 1991–93. –/86. 39.2t.
64809–858. DMSO(B). Lot No. 31100 BREL York 1991–93. –/86. 39.2t.
65734–749. DMSO(A). Lot No. 31103 Metro-Cammell 1991–93. –/86. 39.2t.
65784–799. DMSO(B). Lot No. 31103 Metro-Cammell 1991–93. –/86. 39.2t.
65800–846. DMSO(A). Lot No. 31130 ABB York 1993–94. –/86. 39.2t.
65847–893. DMSO(B). Lot No. 31130 ABB York 1993–94. –/86. 39.2t.
72028–126 (even nos.) TSO. Lot No. 31102 BREL York 1991–93. –/90. 27.2t.
72029–127 (odd nos.) TSO. Lot No. 31101 BREL York 1991–93. –/86 1T. 28.0t.
72787–817 (odd nos.) TSO. Lot No. 31104 Metro-Cammell 1991–92. –/86 1T. 28.0t.
72788–818 (even nos.) TSO. Lot No. 31105 Metro-Cammell 1991–92. –/90. 27.2t.
72900–992 (even nos.) TSO. Lot No. 31102 ABB York 1993–94. –/90. 27.2t.
72901–993 (odd nos.) TSO. Lot No. 31101 ABB York 1993–94. –/86 1T. 28.0t.

Class 465/0. Built by BREL/ABB.

465 001	**SE**	E	*SE*	SG	64759	72028	72029	64809
465 002	**SE**	E	*SE*	SG	64760	72030	72031	64810
465 003	**SE**	E	*SE*	SG	64761	72032	72033	64811
465 004	**SE**	E	*SE*	SG	64762	72034	72035	64812
465 005	**SE**	E	*SE*	SG	64763	72036	72037	64813
465 006	**SE**	E	*SE*	SG	64764	72038	72039	64814
465 007	**SE**	E	*SE*	SG	64765	72040	72041	64815
465 008	**SE**	E	*SE*	SG	64766	72042	72043	64816
465 009	**SE**	E	*SE*	SG	64767	72044	72045	64817
465 010	**SE**	E	*SE*	SG	64768	72046	72047	64818
465 011	**SE**	E	*SE*	SG	64769	72048	72049	64819
465 012	**SE**	E	*SE*	SG	64770	72050	72051	64820
465 013	**SE**	E	*SE*	SG	64771	72052	72053	64821
465 014	**SE**	E	*SE*	SG	64772	72054	72055	64822
465 015	**SE**	E	*SE*	SG	64773	72056	72057	64823
465 016	**SE**	E	*SE*	SG	64774	72058	72059	64824
465 017	**SE**	E	*SE*	SG	64775	72060	72061	64825
465 018	**SE**	E	*SE*	SG	64776	72062	72063	64826
465 019	**SE**	E	*SE*	SG	64777	72064	72065	64827
465 020	**SE**	E	*SE*	SG	64778	72066	72067	64828
465 021	**SE**	E	*SE*	SG	64779	72068	72069	64829
465 022	**SE**	E	*SE*	SG	64780	72070	72071	64830
465 023	**SE**	E	*SE*	SG	64781	72072	72073	64831
465 024	**SE**	E	*SE*	SG	64782	72074	72075	64832
465 025	**SE**	E	*SE*	SG	64783	72076	72077	64833
465 026	**SE**	E	*SE*	SG	64784	72078	72079	64834
465 027	**SE**	E	*SE*	SG	64785	72080	72081	64835
465 028	**SE**	E	*SE*	SG	64786	72082	72083	64836
465 029	**SE**	E	*SE*	SG	64787	72084	72085	64837
465 030	**SE**	E	*SE*	SG	64788	72086	72087	64838
465 031	**SE**	E	*SE*	SG	64789	72088	72089	64839
465 032	**SE**	E	*SE*	SG	64790	72090	72091	64840
465 033	**SE**	E	*SE*	SG	64791	72092	72093	64841
465 034	**SE**	E	*SE*	SG	64792	72094	72095	64842
465 035	**SE**	E	*SE*	SG	64793	72096	72097	64843

465 036	**SE**	E	*SE*	SG	64794	72098	72099	64844
465 037	**SE**	E	*SE*	SG	64795	72100	72101	64845
465 038	**SE**	E	*SE*	SG	64796	72102	72103	64846
465 039	**SE**	E	*SE*	SG	64797	72104	72105	64847
465 040	**SE**	E	*SE*	SG	64798	72106	72107	64848
465 041	**SE**	E	*SE*	SG	64799	72108	72109	64849
465 042	**SE**	E	*SE*	SG	64800	72110	72111	64850
465 043	**SE**	E	*SE*	SG	64801	72112	72113	64851
465 044	**SE**	E	*SE*	SG	64802	72114	72115	64852
465 045	**SE**	E	*SE*	SG	64803	72116	72117	64853
465 046	**SE**	E	*SE*	SG	64804	72118	72119	64854
465 047	**SE**	E	*SE*	SG	64805	72120	72121	64855
465 048	**SE**	E	*SE*	SG	64806	72122	72123	64856
465 049	**SE**	E	*SE*	SG	64807	72124	72125	64857
465 050	**SE**	E	*SE*	SG	64808	72126	72127	64858

Class 465/1. Built by BREL/ABB. Similar to Class 465/0 but with detail differences.

465 151	**SE**	E	*SE*	SG	65800	72900	72901	65847
465 152	**SE**	E	*SE*	SG	65801	72902	72903	65848
465 153	**SE**	E	*SE*	SG	65802	72904	72905	65849
465 154	**SE**	E	*SE*	SG	65803	72906	72907	65850
465 155	**SE**	E	*SE*	SG	65804	72908	72909	65851
465 156	**SE**	E	*SE*	SG	65805	72910	72911	65852
465 157	**SE**	E	*SE*	SG	65806	72912	72913	65853
465 158	**SE**	E	*SE*	SG	65807	72914	72915	65854
465 159	**SE**	E	*SE*	SG	65808	72916	72917	65855
465 160	**SE**	E	*SE*	SG	65809	72918	72919	65856
465 161	**SE**	E	*SE*	SG	65810	72920	72921	65857
465 162	**SE**	E	*SE*	SG	65811	72922	72923	65858
465 163	**SE**	E	*SE*	SG	65812	72924	72925	65859
465 164	**SE**	E	*SE*	SG	65813	72926	72927	65860
465 165	**SE**	E	*SE*	SG	65814	72928	72929	65861
465 166	**SE**	E	*SE*	SG	65815	72930	72931	65862
465 167	**SE**	E	*SE*	SG	65816	72932	72933	65863
465 168	**SE**	E	*SE*	SG	65817	72934	72935	65864
465 169	**SE**	E	*SE*	SG	65818	72936	72937	65865
465 170	**SE**	E	*SE*	SG	65819	72938	72939	65866
465 171	**SE**	E	*SE*	SG	65820	72940	72941	65867
465 172	**SE**	E	*SE*	SG	65821	72942	72943	65868
465 173	**SE**	E	*SE*	SG	65822	72944	72945	65869
465 174	**SE**	E	*SE*	SG	65823	72946	72947	65870
465 175	**SE**	E	*SE*	SG	65824	72948	72949	65871
465 176	**SE**	E	*SE*	SG	65825	72950	72951	65872
465 177	**SE**	E	*SE*	SG	65826	72952	72953	65873
465 178	**SE**	E	*SE*	SG	65827	72954	72955	65874
465 179	**SE**	E	*SE*	SG	65828	72956	72957	65875
465 180	**SE**	E	*SE*	SG	65829	72958	72959	65876
465 181	**SE**	E	*SE*	SG	65830	72960	72961	65877
465 182	**SE**	E	*SE*	SG	65831	72962	72963	65878
465 183	**SE**	E	*SE*	SG	65832	72964	72965	65879
465 184	**SE**	E	*SE*	SG	65833	72966	72967	65880

465 185	**SE**	E	*SE*	SG	65834	72968	72969	65881
465 186	**SE**	E	*SE*	SG	65835	72970	72971	65882
465 187	**SE**	E	*SE*	SG	65836	72972	72973	65883
465 188	**SE**	E	*SE*	SG	65837	72974	72975	65884
465 189	**SE**	E	*SE*	SG	65838	72976	72977	65885
465 190	**SE**	E	*SE*	SG	65839	72978	72979	65886
465 191	**SE**	E	*SE*	SG	65840	72980	72981	65887
465 192	**SE**	E	*SE*	SG	65841	72982	72983	65888
465 193	**SE**	E	*SE*	SG	65842	72984	72985	65889
465 194	**SE**	E	*SE*	SG	65843	72986	72987	65890
465 195	**SE**	E	*SE*	SG	65844	72988	72989	65891
465 196	**SE**	E	*SE*	SG	65845	72990	72991	65892
465 197	**SE**	E	*SE*	SG	65846	72992	72993	65893

Class 465/2. Built by Metro-Cammell. **Dimensions:** 20.80/20.15 x 2.81 m.

* Fitted with universal access toilet to meet the 2020 accessibilty regulations. Full details awaited.

465 235		**SE**	A	*SE*	SG	65734	72787	72788	65784
465 236		**SE**	A	*SE*	SG	65735	72789	72790	65785
465 237		**SE**	A	*SE*	SG	65736	72791	72792	65786
465 238	*	**SE**	A	*SE*	SG	65737	72793	72794	65787
465 239		**SE**	A	*SE*	SG	65738	72795	72796	65788
465 240		**SE**	A	*SE*	SG	65739	72797	72798	65789
465 241		**SE**	A	*SE*	SG	65740	72799	72800	65790
465 242	*	**SE**	A	*SE*	SG	65741	72801	72802	65791
465 243		**SE**	A	*SE*	SG	65742	72803	72804	65792
465 244		**SE**	A	*SE*	SG	65743	72805	72806	65793
465 245		**SE**	A	*SE*	SG	65744	72807	72808	65794
465 246		**SE**	A	*SE*	SG	65745	72809	72810	65795
465 247		**SE**	A	*SE*	SG	65746	72811	72812	65796
465 248		**SE**	A	*SE*	SG	65747	72813	72814	65797
465 249		**SE**	A	*SE*	SG	65748	72815	72816	65798
465 250		**SE**	A	*SE*	SG	65749	72817	72818	65799

Class 465/9. Built by Metro-Cammell. Refurbished 2005 for longer distance services, with the addition of First Class. Details as Class 465/0 unless stated.
Formation: DMCO–TSO(A)–TSO(B)–DMCO.
Seating Layout: 1: 2+2 facing/unidirectional, 2: 3+2 facing/unidirectional.

* Fitted with universal access toilet to meet the 2020 accessibilty regulations.

65700–733. DMCO(A). Lot No. 31103 Metro-Cammell 1991–93. 12/68. 39.2 t.
72719–785 (odd nos.) TSO(A). Lot No. 31104 Metro-Cammell 1991–92. –/76 1T 2W (* –/65(+7) 1TD 2W). 30.3 t.
72720–786 (even nos.) TSO(B). Lot No. 31105 Metro-Cammell 1991–92. –/90. 29.5 t.
65750–783. DMCO(B). Lot No. 31103 Metro-Cammell 1991–93. 12/68. 39.2 t.

465 901	(465 201)		**SE**	A	*SE*	SG	65700	72719	72720	65750
465 902	(465 202)		**SE**	A	*SE*	SG	65701	72721	72722	65751
465 903	(465 203)		**SE**	A	*SE*	SG	65702	72723	72724	65752
465 904	(465 204)		**SE**	A	*SE*	SG	65703	72725	72726	65753
465 905	(465 205)	*	**SE**	A	*SE*	SG	65704	72727	72728	65754

465 906	(465 206)	*	**SE**	A	*SE*	SG	65705	72729 72730	65755
465 907	(465 207)	*	**SE**	A	*SE*	SG	65706	72731 72732	65756
465 908	(465 208)	*	**SE**	A	*SE*	SG	65707	72733 72734	65757
465 909	(465 209)	*	**SE**	A	*SE*	SG	65708	72735 72736	65758
465 910	(465 210)	*	**SE**	A	*SE*	SG	65709	72737 72738	65759
465 911	(465 211)		**SE**	A	*SE*	SG	65710	72739 72740	65760
465 912	(465 212)		**SE**	A	*SE*	SG	65711	72741 72742	65761
465 913	(465 213)	*	**SE**	A	*SE*	SG	65712	72743 72744	65762
465 914	(465 214)	*	**SE**	A	*SE*	SG	65713	72745 72746	65763
465 915	(465 215)		**SE**	A	*SE*	SG	65714	72747 72748	65764
465 916	(465 216)	*	**SE**	A	*SE*	SG	65715	72749 72750	65765
465 917	(465 217)		**SE**	A	*SE*	SG	65716	72751 72752	65766
465 918	(465 218)		**SE**	A	*SE*	SG	65717	72753 72754	65767
465 919	(465 219)		**SE**	A	*SE*	SG	65718	72755 72756	65768
465 920	(465 220)		**SE**	A	*SE*	SG	65719	72757 72758	65769
465 921	(465 221)	*	**SE**	A	*SE*	SG	65720	72759 72760	65770
465 922	(465 222)		**SE**	A	*SE*	SG	65721	72761 72762	65771
465 923	(465 223)	*	**SE**	A	*SE*	SG	65722	72763 72764	65772
465 924	(465 224)	*	**SE**	A	*SE*	SG	65723	72765 72766	65773
465 925	(465 225)		**SE**	A	*SE*	SG	65724	72767 72768	65774
465 926	(465 226)		**SE**	A	*SE*	SG	65725	72769 72770	65775
465 927	(465 227)		**SE**	A	*SE*	SG	65726	72771 72772	65776
465 928	(465 228)		**SE**	A	*SE*	SG	65727	72773 72774	65777
465 929	(465 229)		**SE**	A	*SE*	SG	65728	72775 72776	65778
465 930	(465 230)		**SE**	A	*SE*	SG	65729	72777 72778	65779
465 931	(465 231)		**SE**	A	*SE*	SG	65730	72779 72780	65780
465 932	(465 232)		**SE**	A	*SE*	SG	65731	72781 72782	65781
465 933	(465 233)	*	**SE**	A	*SE*	SG	65732	72783 72784	65782
465 934	(465 234)	*	**SE**	A	*SE*	SG	65733	72785 72786	65783

CLASS 466   NETWORKER   GEC-ALSTHOM

Inner/outer suburban units.

Formation: DMSO–DTSO.
Construction: Welded aluminium alloy.
Traction Motors: Two GEC-Alsthom G352AY asynchronous of 280kW.
Wheel Arrangement: Bo-Bo + 2-2.   **Couplers:** Tightlock.
Braking: Disc, rheostatic & regen.   **Control System:** 1992-type GTO Inverter.
Dimensions: 20.80 x 2.80 m.   **Maximum Speed:** 75 mph.
Bogies: BREL P3/T3.   **Doors:** Sliding plug.
Gangways: Within unit.   **Seating Layout:** 3+2 facing/unidirectional.
Multiple Working: Within class and with Class 465.

DMSO. Lot No. 31128 Birmingham 1993–94. –/86. 40.6t.
DTSO. Lot No. 31129 Birmingham 1993–94. –/82 1T. 31.4t.

466 001	**SE**	A	*SE*	SG	64860	78312
466 002	**SE**	A	*SE*	SG	64861	78313
466 003	**SE**	A	*SE*	SG	64862	78314
466 004	**SE**	A	*SE*	SG	64863	78315
466 005	**SE**	A	*SE*	SG	64864	78316

466006	**SE**	A	*SE*	SG	64865	78317
466007	**SE**	A	*SE*	SG	64866	78318
466008	**SE**	A	*SE*	SG	64867	78319
466009	**SE**	A	*SE*	SG	64868	78320
466010	**SE**	A	*SE*	SG	64869	78321
466011	**SE**	A	*SE*	SG	64870	78322
466012	**SE**	A	*SE*	SG	64871	78323
466013	**SE**	A	*SE*	SG	64872	78324
466014	**SE**	A	*SE*	SG	64873	78325
466015	**SE**	A	*SE*	SG	64874	78326
466016	**SE**	A	*SE*	SG	64875	78327
466017	**SE**	A	*SE*	SG	64876	78328
466018	**SE**	A	*SE*	SG	64877	78329
466019	**SE**	A	*SE*	SG	64878	78330
466020	**SE**	A	*SE*	SG	64879	78332
466021	**SE**	A	*SE*	SG	64880	78332
466022	**SE**	A	*SE*	SG	64881	78333
466023	**SE**	A	*SE*	SG	64882	78334
466024	**SE**	A	*SE*	SG	64883	78335
466025	**SE**	A	*SE*	SG	64884	78336
466026	**SE**	A	*SE*	SG	64885	78337
466027	**SE**	A	*SE*	SG	64886	78338
466028	**SE**	A	*SE*	SG	64887	78339
466029	**SE**	A	*SE*	SG	64888	78340
466030	**SE**	A	*SE*	SG	64889	78341
466031	**SE**	A	*SE*	SG	64890	78342
466032	**SE**	A	*SE*	SG	64891	78343
466033	**SE**	A	*SE*	SG	64892	78344
466034	**SE**	A	*SE*	SG	64893	78345
466035	**SE**	A	*SE*	SG	64894	78346
466036	**SE**	A	*SE*	SG	64895	78347
466037	**SE**	A	*SE*	SG	64896	78348
466038	**SE**	A	*SE*	SG	64897	78349
466039	**SE**	A	*SE*	SG	64898	78350
466040	**SE**	A	*SE*	SG	64899	78351
466041	**SE**	A	*SE*	SG	64900	78352
466042	**SE**	A	*SE*	SG	64901	78353
466043	**SE**	A	*SE*	SG	64902	78354

CLASS 483   METRO-CAMMELL

Built 1938 onwards for LTE. Converted 1989–90 for the Isle of Wight Line.

Formation: DMSO–DMSO.
System: 660 V DC third rail.
Construction: Steel.
Traction Motors: Two Crompton Parkinson/GEC/BTH LT100 of 125 kW.
Braking: Tread.   **Dimensions:** 16.15 x 2.69 m.
Bogies: LT design.   **Couplers:** Wedglock.
Gangways: None. End doors.
Control System: Pneumatic Camshaft Motor (PCM).
Doors: Sliding.   **Maximum Speed:** 45 mph.
Seating Layout: Longitudinal or 2+2 facing/unidirectional.
Multiple Working: Within class.
The last three numbers of the unit number only are carried.

Former London Underground numbers are shown in parentheses.

DMSO (A). Lot No. 31071. –/40. 27.4 t.
DMSO (B). Lot No. 31072. –/42. 27.4 t.

483 002	**LT**	SW		RY (S)	122	(10221)	225	(11142)	RAPTOR
483 004	**LT**	SW	*SW*	RY	124	(10205)	224	(11205)	
483 006	**LT**	SW	*SW*	RY	126	(10297)	226	(11297)	
483 007	**LT**	SW	*SW*	RY	127	(10291)	227	(11291)	
483 008	**LT**	SW	*SW*	RY	128	(10255)	228	(11255)	
483 009	**LT**	SW	*SW*	RY	129	(10229)	229	(11229)	

CLASS 507   BREL YORK

Formation: BDMSO–TSO–DMSO.
Construction: Steel underframe, aluminium alloy body and roof.
Traction Motors: Four GEC G310AZ of 82.125 kW.
Wheel Arrangement: Bo-Bo + 2-2 + Bo-Bo.
Braking: Disc & rheostatic.   **Dimensions:** 20.18 x 2.82 m.
Bogies: BX1.   **Couplers:** Tightlock.
Gangways: Within unit + end doors. **Control System:** Camshaft.
Doors: Sliding.   **Maximum Speed:** 75 mph.
Seating Layout: All refurbished with 2+2 high-back facing seating.
Multiple Working: Within class and with Class 508.

Advertising livery: 507 002 Liverpool Hope University (white).

BDMSO. Lot No. 30906 1978–80. –/56(+3) 1W. 37.0 t.
TSO. Lot No. 30907 1978–80. –/74. 25.5 t.
DMSO. Lot No. 30908 1978–80. –/56(+3) 1W. 35.5 t.

507 001	**MY**	A	*ME*	BD	64367	71342	64405
507 002	**AL**	A	*ME*	BD	64368	71343	64406
507 003	**MY**	A	*ME*	BD	64369	71344	64407
507 004	**MY**	A	*ME*	BD	64388	71345	64408
507 005	**MY**	A	*ME*	BD	64371	71346	64409

507 006	**MY**	A	*ME*	BD	64372	71347	64410
507 007	**MY**	A	*ME*	BD	64373	71348	64411
507 008	**MY**	A	*ME*	BD	64374	71349	64412
507 009	**MY**	A	*ME*	BD	64375	71350	64413
507 010	**MY**	A	*ME*	BD	64376	71351	64414
507 011	**MY**	A	*ME*	BD	64377	71352	64415
507 012	**MY**	A	*ME*	BD	64378	71353	64416
507 013	**MY**	A	*ME*	BD	64379	71354	64417
507 014	**MY**	A	*ME*	BD	64380	71355	64418
507 015	**MY**	A	*ME*	BD	64381	71356	64419
507 016	**MY**	A	*ME*	BD	64382	71357	64420
507 017	**MY**	A	*ME*	BD	64383	71358	64421
507 018	**MY**	A	*ME*	BD	64384	71359	64422
507 019	**MY**	A	*ME*	BD	64385	71360	64423
507 020	**MY**	A	*ME*	BD	64386	71361	64424
507 021	**MY**	A	*ME*	BD	64387	71362	64425
507 023	**MY**	A	*ME*	BD	64389	71364	64427
507 024	**MY**	A	*ME*	BD	64390	71365	64428
507 025	**MY**	A	*ME*	BD	64391	71366	64429
507 026	**MY**	A	*ME*	BD	64392	71367	64430
507 027	**MY**	A	*ME*	BD	64393	71368	64431
507 028	**MY**	A	*ME*	BD	64394	71369	64432
507 029	**MY**	A	*ME*	BD	64395	71370	64433
507 030	**MY**	A	*ME*	BD	64396	71371	64434
507 031	**MY**	A	*ME*	BD	64397	71372	64435
507 032	**MY**	A	*ME*	BD	64398	71373	64436
507 033	**MY**	A	*ME*	BD	64399	71374	64437

Names:

507 004 Bob Paisley
507 008 Harold Wilson
507 009 Dixie Dean
507 016 Merseyrail – celebrating the first ten years (2003–2013)
507 020 John Peel
507 021 Red Rum
507 023 Operations Inspector Stuart Mason
507 026 Councillor George Howard
507 033 Councillor Jack Spriggs

CLASS 508   BREL YORK

Formation: DMSO–TSO–BDMSO.
Construction: Steel underframe, aluminium alloy body and roof.
Traction Motors: Four GEC G310AZ of 82.125 kW.
Wheel Arrangement: Bo-Bo + 2-2 + Bo-Bo.
Braking: Disc & rheostatic.   **Dimensions:** 20.18 x 2.82 m.
Bogies: BX1.   **Couplers:** Tightlock.
Gangways: Within unit + end doors. **Control System:** Camshaft.
Doors: Sliding.   **Maximum Speed:** 75 mph.
Seating Layout: All refurbished with 2+2 high-back facing seating.
Multiple Working: Within class and with Class 507.

Advertising livery: 508 111 Beatles Story (blue).

DMSO. Lot No. 30979 1979–80. –/56(+3) 1W. 36.0 t.
TSO. Lot No. 30980 1979–80. –/74. 26.5 t.
BDMSO. Lot No. 30981 1979–80. –/56(+3) 1W. 36.5 t.

508 103	**MY**	A	*ME*	BD	64651	71485	64694
508 104	**MY**	A	*ME*	BD	64652	71486	64695
508 108	**MY**	A	*ME*	BD	64656	71490	64699
508 110	**MY**	A	*ME*	BD	64658	71492	64701
508 111	**AL**	A	*ME*	BD	64659	71493	64702
508 112	**MY**	A	*ME*	BD	64660	71494	64703
508 114	**MY**	A	*ME*	BD	64662	71496	64705
508 115	**MY**	A	*ME*	BD	64663	71497	64706
508 117	**MY**	A	*ME*	BD	64665	71499	64708
508 120	**MY**	A	*ME*	BD	64668	71502	64711
508 122	**MY**	A	*ME*	BD	64670	71504	64713
508 123	**MY**	A	*ME*	BD	64671	71505	64714
508 124	**MY**	A	*ME*	BD	64672	71506	64715
508 125	**MY**	A	*ME*	BD	64673	71507	64716
508 126	**MY**	A	*ME*	BD	64674	71508	64717
508 127	**MY**	A	*ME*	BD	64675	71509	64718
508 128	**MY**	A	*ME*	BD	64676	71510	64719
508 130	**MY**	A	*ME*	BD	64678	71512	64721
508 131	**MY**	A	*ME*	BD	64679	71513	64722
508 134	**MY**	A	*ME*	BD	64682	71516	64725
508 136	**MY**	A	*ME*	BD	64684	71518	64727
508 137	**MY**	A	*ME*	BD	64685	71519	64728
508 138	**MY**	A	*ME*	BD	64686	71520	64729
508 139	**MY**	A	*ME*	BD	64687	71521	64730
508 140	**MY**	A	*ME*	BD	64688	71522	64731
508 141	**MY**	A	*ME*	BD	64689	71523	64732
508 143	**MY**	A	*ME*	BD	64691	71525	64734

Names:

508 111 The Beatles
508 123 William Roscoe
508 136 Wilfred Owen MC

3. DUAL-VOLTAGE UNITS

Initially the Class 7xx EMU series was reserved for Siemens "Desiro City" units, but it has now been announced that the new Bombardier units for London Overground will be Class 710s (full number series to be confirmed). The Class 7xx series is being used for EMUs as freight wagons take up many of the remaining potential Class 3xx series'.

CLASS 700   DESIRO CITY   SIEMENS

The Class 700s are a large fleet of EMUs currently entering service with Govia Thameslink. The first unit was delivered in summer 2015, the first entered traffic in spring 2016 and all units will be in traffic the end of 2018. The units are being financed by Cross London Trains (a consortium of Siemens Project Ventures, Innisfree Ltd and 3i Infrastructure Ltd).

Formations (8-car): DMCO–PTSO–MSO–TSO–TSO–MSO–PTSO–DMCO
or **(12-car):** DMCO–PTSO–MSO–MSO–TSO–TSO–TSO–TSO–MSO–MSO–PTSO–DMCO.
Systems: 25 kV AC overhead/750 V DC third rail.
Construction: Aluminium.
Traction Motors: 4 Siemens asynchronous of 200 kW.
Wheel Arrangement (8-car): Bo-Bo + 2-2 + Bo-Bo + 2-2 + 2-2 + Bo-Bo + 2-2 + Bo-Bo. **(12-car):** Bo-Bo + 2-2 + Bo-Bo + Bo-Bo + 2-2 + 2-2 + 2-2 + 2-2 + Bo-Bo + Bo-Bo + 2-2 + Bo-Bo.
Braking: Disc & regenerative   **Dimensions:** 20.00/20.16 m x 2.80 m.
Bogies: Siemens SF7000 inside-frame. **Couplers:** Dellner 12.
Gangways: Within unit.   **Control System:** IGBT Inverter.
Doors: Sliding plug.   **Maximum Speed:** 100 mph.
Heating & ventilation: Air conditioning.
Seating Layout: 2+2 facing/unidirectional.
Multiple Working: Within class and with Class 707.

Class 700/0. 8-car units.

DMCO(A). Siemens Krefeld 2014–18. 26/16(+3).   t.
PTSO. Siemens Krefeld 2014–18. –/54 1T.   t.
MSO. Siemens Krefeld 2014–18. –/64.   t.
TSO. Siemens Krefeld 2014–18. –/56.   t.
TSO(W). Siemens Krefeld 2014–18. –/40(+8) 1TD 2W.   t.
MSO. Siemens Krefeld 2014–18. –/64.   t.
PTSO. Siemens Krefeld 2014–18. –/54 1T.   t.
DMCO(B). Siemens Krefeld 2014–18. 26/16(+3).   t.

700001	**TL** CL			401001	402001	403001	406001
				407001	410001	411001	412001
700002	**TL** CL	*TL*	TB	401002	402002	403002	406002
				407002	410002	411002	412002
700003	**TL** CL	*TL*	TB	401003	402003	403003	406003
				407003	410003	411003	412003
700004	**TL** CL		TB	401004	402004	403004	406004
				407004	410004	411004	412004

700 005	**TL** CL		TB	401005	402005	403005	406005
				407005	410005	411005	412005
700 006	**TL** CL		TB	401006	402006	403006	406006
				407006	410006	411006	412006
700 007	**TL** CL		TB	401007	402007	403007	406007
				407007	410007	411007	412007
700 008	**TL** CL	*TL*	TB	401008	402008	403008	406008
				407008	410008	411008	412008
700 009	**TL** CL			401009	402009	403009	406009
				407009	410009	411009	412009
700 010	**TL** CL	*TL*	TB	401010	402010	403010	406010
				407010	410010	411010	412010
700 011	**TL** CL			401011	402011	403011	406011
				407011	410011	411011	412011
700 012	**TL** CL			401012	402012	403012	406012
				407012	410012	411012	412012
700 013	**TL** CL			401013	402013	403013	406013
				407013	410013	411013	412013
700 014	**TL** CL		TB	401014	402014	403014	406014
				407014	410014	411014	412014
700 015	**TL** CL		TB	401015	402015	403015	406015
				407015	410015	411015	412015
700 016	**TL** CL		TB	401016	402016	403016	406016
				407016	410016	411016	412016
700 017	**TL** CL			401017	402017	403017	406017
				407017	410017	411017	412017
700 018	**TL** CL		TB	401018	402018	403018	406018
				407018	410018	411018	412018
700 019	**TL** CL	*TL*	TB	401019	402019	403019	406019
				407019	410019	411019	412019
700 020	**TL** CL		TB	401020	402020	403020	406020
				407020	410020	411020	412020
700 021	**TL** CL		TB	401021	402021	403021	406021
				407021	410021	411021	412021
700 022	**TL** CL			401022	402022	403022	406022
				407022	410022	411022	412022
700 023	**TL** CL			401023	402023	403023	406023
				407023	410023	411023	412023
700 024	**TL** CL			401024	402024	403024	406024
				407024	410024	411024	412024
700 025	**TL** CL			401025	402025	403025	406025
				407025	410025	411025	412025
700 026	**TL** CL			401026	402026	403026	406026
				407026	410026	411026	412026
700 027	**TL** CL			401027	402027	403027	406027
				407027	410027	411027	412027
700 028	**TL** CL			401028	402028	403028	406028
				407028	410028	411028	412028
700 029	**TL** CL			401029	402029	403029	406029
				407029	410029	411029	412029

700 030	**TL** CL	401030	402030	403030	406030	
		407030	410030	411030	412030	
700 031	**TL** CL	401031	402031	403031	406031	
		407031	410031	411031	412031	
700 032	**TL** CL	401032	402032	403032	406032	
		407032	410032	411032	412032	
700 033	**TL** CL	401033	402033	403033	406033	
		407033	410033	411033	412033	
700 034	**TL** CL	401034	402034	403034	406034	
		407034	410034	411034	412034	
700 035	**TL** CL	401035	402035	403035	406035	
		407035	410035	411035	412035	
700 036	**TL** CL	401036	402036	403036	406036	
		407036	410036	411036	412036	
700 037	**TL** CL	401037	402037	403037	406037	
		407037	410037	411037	412037	
700 038	**TL** CL	401038	402038	403038	406038	
		407038	410038	411038	412038	
700 039	**TL** CL	401039	402039	403039	406039	
		407039	410039	411039	412039	
700 040	**TL** CL	401040	402040	403040	406040	
		407040	410040	411040	412040	
700 041	**TL** CL	401041	402041	403041	406041	
		407041	410041	411041	412041	
700 042	**TL** CL	401042	402042	403042	406042	
		407042	410042	411042	412042	
700 043	**TL** CL	401043	402043	403043	406043	
		407043	410043	411043	412043	
700 044	**TL** CL	401044	402044	403044	406044	
		407044	410044	411044	412044	
700 045	**TL** CL	401045	402045	403045	406045	
		407045	410045	411045	412045	
700 046	**TL** CL	401046	402046	403046	406046	
		407046	410046	411046	412046	
700 047	**TL** CL	401047	402047	403047	406047	
		407047	410047	411047	412047	
700 048	**TL** CL	401048	402048	403048	406048	
		407048	410048	411048	412048	
700 049	**TL** CL	401049	402049	403049	406049	
		407049	410049	411049	412049	
700 050	**TL** CL	401050	402050	403050	406050	
		407050	410050	411050		
700 051	**TL** CL	401051	402051	403051	406051	
		407051	410051	411051	412051	
700 052	**TL** CL	401052	402052	403052	406052	
		407052	410052	411052	412052	
700 053	**TL** CL	401053	402053	403053	406053	
		407053	410053	411053	412053	
700 054	**TL** CL	401054	402054	403054	406054	
		407054	410054	411054	412054	

700055	**TL** CL			401055	402055	403055	406055
				407055	410055	411055	412055
700056	**TL** CL			401056	402056	403056	406056
				407056	410056	411056	412056
700057	**TL** CL			401057	402057	403057	406057
				407057	410057	411057	412057
700058	**TL** CL			401058	402058	403058	406058
				407058	410058	411058	412058
700059	**TL** CL			401059	402059	403059	406059
				407059	410059	411059	412059
700060	**TL** CL			401060	402060	403060	406060
				407060	410060	411060	412060

Class 700/1. 12-car units.

DMCO(A). Siemens Krefeld 2013–18. 26/20. 38.4 t.
PTSO. Siemens Krefeld 2013–18. –/54 1T. 34.5 t.
MSO. Siemens Krefeld 2013–18. –/60(+3). 36.2 t.
MSO. Siemens Krefeld 2013–18. –/56 1T. 35.8 t.
TSO. Siemens Krefeld 2013–18. –/64. 26.9 t.
TSO. Siemens Krefeld 2013–18. –/56. 28.6 t.
TSO(W). Siemens Krefeld 2013–18. –/37(+8) 1TD 2W. 29.0 t.
TSO. Siemens Krefeld 2013–18. –/64. 28.2 t.
MSO. Siemens Krefeld 2013–18. –/56 1T. 35.8 t.
MSO. Siemens Krefeld 2013–18. –/60(+3). 36.2 t.
PTSO. Siemens Krefeld 2013–18. –/54 1T. 34.5 t.
DMCO(B). Siemens Krefeld 2013–18. 26/20. 38.5 t.

700101	**TL** CL		TB	401101	402101	403101	404101	405101	406101
				407101	408101	409101	410101	411101	412101
700102	**TL** CL *TL*	TB	401102	402102	403102	404102	405102	406102
				407102	408102	409102	410102	411102	412102
700103	**TL** CL *TL*	TB	401103	402103	403103	404103	405103	406103
				407103	408103	409103	410103	411103	412103
700104	**TL** CL *TL*	TB	401104	402104	403104	404104	405104	406104
				407104	408104	409104	410104	411104	412104
700105	**TL** CL		TB	401105	402105	403105	404105	405105	406105
				407105	408105	409105	410105	411105	412105
700106	**TL** CL *TL*	TB	401106	402106	403106	404106	405106	406106
				407106	408106	409106	410106	411106	412106
700107	**TL** CL *TL*	TB	401107	402107	403107	404107	405107	406107
				407107	408107	409107	410107	411107	412107
700108	**TL** CL *TL*	TB	401108	402108	403108	404108	405108	406108
				407108	408108	409108	410108	411108	412108
700109	**TL** CL *TL*	TB	401109	402109	403109	404109	405109	406109
				407109	408109	409109	410109	411109	412109
700110	**TL** CL *TL*	TB	401110	402110	403110	404110	405110	406110
				407110	408110	409110	410110	411110	412110
700111	**TL** CL *TL*	TB	401111	402111	403111	404111	405111	406111
				407111	408111	409111	410111	411111	412111
700112	**TL** CL *TL*	TB	401112	402112	403112	404112	405112	406112
				407112	408112	409112	410112	411112	412112

700 113	**TL** CL *TL*	TB	401113 402113 403113 404113 405113 406113
			407113 408113 409113 410113 411113 412113
700 114	**TL** CL *TL*	TB	401114 402114 403114 404114 405114 406114
			407114 408114 409114 410114 411114 412114
700 115	**TL** CL	TB	401115 402115 403115 404115 405115 406115
			407115 408115 409115 410115 411115 412115
700 116	**TL** CL		401116 402116 403116 404116 405116 406116
			407116 408116 409116 410116 411116 412116
700 117	**TL** CL		401117 402117 403117 404117 405117 406117
			407117 408117 409117 410117 411117 412117
700 118	**TL** CL		401118 402118 403118 404118 405118 406118
			407118 408118 409118 410118 411118 412118
700 119	**TL** CL		401119 402119 403119 404119 405119 406119
			407119 408119 409119 410119 411119 412119
700 120	**TL** CL		401120 402120 403120 404120 405120 406120
			407120 408120 409120 410120 411120 412120
700 121	**TL** CL		401121 402121 403121 404121 405121 406121
			407121 408121 409121 410121 411121 412121
700 122	**TL** CL		401122 402122 403122 404122 405122 406122
			407122 408122 409122 410122 411122 412122
700 123	**TL** CL		401123 402123 403123 404123 405123 406123
			407123 408123 409123 410123 411123 412123
700 124	**TL** CL		401124 402124 403124 404124 405124 406124
			407124 408124 409124 410124 411124 412124
700 125	**TL** CL		401125 402125 403125 404125 405125 406125
			407125 408125 409125 410125 411125 412125
700 126	**TL** CL		401126 402126 403126 404126 405126 406126
			407126 408126 409126 410126 411126 412126
700 127	**TL** CL		401127 402127 403127 404127 405127 406127
			407127 408127 409127 410127 411127 412127
700 128	**TL** CL		401128 402128 403128 404128 405128 406128
			407128 408128 409128 410128 411128 412128
700 129	**TL** CL		401129 402129 403129 404129 405129 406129
			407129 408129 409129 410129 411129 412129
700 130	**TL** CL		401130 402130 403130 404130 405130 406130
			407130 408130 409130 410130 411130 412130
700 131	**TL** CL		401131 402131 403131 404131 405131 406131
			407131 408131 409131 410131 411131 412131
700 132	**TL** CL		401132 402132 403132 404132 405132 406132
			407132 408132 409132 410132 411132 412132
700 133	**TL** CL		401133 402133 403133 404133 405133 406133
			407133 408133 409133 410133 411133 412133
700 134	**TL** CL		401134 402134 403134 404134 405134 406134
			407134 408134 409134 410134 411134 412134
700 135	**TL** CL		401135 402135 403135 404135 405135 406135
			407135 408135 409135 410135 411135 412135
700 136	**TL** CL		401136 402136 403136 404136 405136 406136
			407136 408136 409136 410136 411136 412136
700 137	**TL** CL		401137 402137 403137 404137 405137 406137
			407137 408137 409137 410137 411137 412137

700 138	**TL** CL		401138	402138	403138	404138	405138	406138
			407138	408138	409138	410138	411138	412138
700 139	**TL** CL		401139	402139	403139	404139	405139	406139
			407139	408139	409139	410139	411139	412139
700 140	**TL** CL		401140	402140	403140	404140	405140	406140
			407140	408140	409140	410140	411140	412140
700 141	**TL** CL		401141	402141	403141	404141	405141	406141
			407141	408141	409141	410141	411141	412141
700 142	**TL** CL		401142	402142	403142	404142	405142	406142
			407142	408142	409142	410142	411142	412142
700 143	**TL** CL		401143	402143	403143	404143	405143	406143
			407143	408143	409143	410143	411143	412143
700 144	**TL** CL		401144	402144	403144	404144	405144	406144
			407144	408144	409144	410144	411144	412144
700 145	**TL** CL		401145	402145	403145	404145	405145	406145
			407145	408145	409145	410145	411145	412145
700 146	**TL** CL		401146	402146	403146	404146	405146	406146
			407146	408146	409146	410146	411146	412146
700 147	**TL** CL		401147	402147	403147	404147	405147	406147
			407147	408147	409147	410147	411147	412147
700 148	**TL** CL		401148	402148	403148	404148	405148	406148
			407148	408148	409148	410148	411148	412148
700 149	**TL** CL		401149	402149	403149	404149	405149	406149
			407149	408149	409149	410149	411149	412149
700 150	**TL** CL		401150	402150	403150	404150	405150	406150
			407150	408150	409150	410150	411150	412150
700 151	**TL** CL		401151	402151	403151	404151	405151	406151
			407151	408151	409151	410151	411151	412151
700 152	**TL** CL		401152	402152	403152	404152	405152	406152
			407152	408152	409152	410152	411152	412152
700 153	**TL** CL		401153	402153	403153	404153	405153	406153
			407153	408153	409153	410153	411153	412153
700 154	**TL** CL		401154	402154	403154	404154	405154	406154
			407154	408154	409154	410154	411154	412154
700 155	**TL** CL		401155	402155	403155	404155	405155	406155
			407155	408155	409155	410155	411155	412155

CLASS 707   DESIRO CITY   SIEMENS

These 30 5-car units are under construction for South West Trains suburban services, with the first unit due to enter traffic in spring 2017. Although they will be planned for use only on third rail DC lines, they will be constructed as dual-voltage units.

Formations: DMSO–PTSO–TSO–TSO–DMSO.
Systems: 25 kV AC overhead/750 V DC third rail.
Construction: Aluminium.
Traction Motors: 4 Siemens asynchronous of 200 kW.
Wheel Arrangement: Bo-Bo + 2-2 + 2-2 + 2-2 + Bo-Bo.
Braking: Disc & regenerative   **Dimensions:** 20.00/20.16 m x 2.80 m.
Bogies: Siemens SF7000 inside-frame. **Couplers:** Dellner 12

Gangways: Within unit.   **Control System:** IGBT Inverter.
Doors: Sliding plug.   **Maximum Speed:** 100 mph.
Heating & ventilation: Air conditioning.
Seating Layout: 2+2/2+1 facing/unidirectional.
Multiple Working: Within class and with Class 700.

DMSO(A). Siemens Krefeld 2015–17. –/46.   t.
PTSO. Siemens Krefeld 2015–17. –/64.   t.
TSO. Siemens Krefeld 2015–17. –/53(+4) 2W.   t.
TSO. Siemens Krefeld 2015–17. –/62.   t.
DMSO(B). Siemens Krefeld 2015–17. –/46.   t.

707 001	**SS**	A	421001	422001	423001	424001	425001
707 002	**SS**	A	421002	422002	423002	424002	425002
707 003	**SS**	A	421003	422003	423003	424003	425003
707 004	**SS**	A	421004	422004	423004	424004	425004
707 005	**SS**	A	421005	422005	423005	424005	425005
707 006	**SS**	A	421006	422006	423006	424006	425006
707 007	**SS**	A	421007	422007	423007	424007	425007
707 008	**SS**	A	421008	422008	423008	424008	425008
707 009	**SS**	A	421009	422009	423009	424009	425009
707 010	**SS**	A	421010	422010	423010	424010	425010
707 011	**SS**	A	421011	422011	423011	424011	425011
707 012	**SS**	A	421012	422012	423012	424012	425012
707 013	**SS**	A	421013	422013	423013	424013	425013
707 014	**SS**	A	421014	422014	423014	424014	425014
707 015	**SS**	A	421015	422015	423015	424015	425015
707 016	**SS**	A	421016	422016	423016	424016	425016
707 017	**SS**	A	421017	422017	423017	424017	425017
707 018	**SS**	A	421018	422018	423018	424018	425018
707 019	**SS**	A	421019	422019	423019	424019	425019
707 020	**SS**	A	421020	422020	423020	424020	425020
707 021	**SS**	A	421021	422021	423021	424021	425021
707 022	**SS**	A	421022	422022	423022	424022	425022
707 023	**SS**	A	421023	422023	423023	424023	425023
707 024	**SS**	A	421024	422024	423024	424024	425024
707 025	**SS**	A	421025	422025	423025	424025	425025
707 026	**SS**	A	421026	422026	423026	424026	425026
707 027	**SS**	A	421027	422027	423027	424027	425027
707 028	**SS**	A	421028	422028	423028	424028	425028
707 029	**SS**	A	421029	422029	423029	424029	425029
707 030	**SS**	A	421030	422030	423030	424030	425030

4. HITACHI IEP UNITS

CLASS 800 INTERCITY EXPRESS PROGRAMME
BI-MODE   HITACHI

In summer 2012 Agility Trains, a consortium of Hitachi and John Laing, signed a deal with the DfT to design, build, finance and maintain the next generation of InterCity rolling stock for the Great Western and East Coast Main Lines, principally to replace ageing High Speed Trains on these routes. A follow-on order in 2013 confirmed that a further 30 9-car trains would be ordered to replace the Class 91s and Mark 4 carriages on the ECML. This brought the total number of vehicles ordered to 866. Both Great Western Railway and Virgin Trains East Coast will have a mix of 5-car and 9-car units which are bi-mode and straight electric trains, although the EMUs will also have one diesel engine fitted to each set. Engines are being supplied by MTU. Owing to delays with electrification works on the Great Western Main Line, in 2016 it was announced that the 21 9-car electric Class 801 units for GWR would be built as 21 9-car bi-mode units, numbered instead in the Class 800/3 series.

The units are broadly based on the Southeastern Class 395 EMUs, but have 26 m length bodyshells. They are numbered in the Class 800 (bi-mode) and Class 801 (EMU) number series'. 12 trains (76 vehicles) are being fully manufactured in Japan before the new Hitachi factory at Newton Aycliffe, County Durham is up and running. The remaining trains will be assembled at Newton Aycliffe. New maintenance depots are being constructed at Stoke Gifford (Bristol), Swansea and North Pole (London, the former Eurostar depot) for the GWR sets and at Doncaster for the VTEC sets.

The first trains arrived for testing in 2015. They will enter service on the Great Western Main Line from spring 2017 and on the East Coast Main Line from 2018.

In 2015 GWR ordered a further 22 5-car and seven 9-car IEPs, to be designated Class 802 (5-car) and Class 802/1 (9-car). These will be used on Paddington–West of England services. In 2016 GWR ordered a further seven 9-car Class 802s, and TransPennine Express ordered 19 5-car Class 802s for delivery 2019–20. As they will predominately operate on diesel power, on these units the engines will run at 700 kW at all times, rather than the Class 800s which will run at 560 kW in normal operation. The GWR Class 802s will be constructed in Pistoia, Italy (the former AnsaldoBreda factory) and the TPE Class 802s at Newton Aycliffe. The number series for the Class 802s has yet to be confirmed.

Formations: Various, see class headings for details.
Systems: Diesel/25 kV AC overhead electric.
Construction: Aluminium.
Engines: MTU 12V 1600 R80L of 700 kW (940 hp). Normally derated to 560 kW.
Traction Motors: Four Hitachi asynchronous of 226 kW.

Wheel Arrangement: 2-2 + Bo-Bo + Bo-Bo + Bo-Bo + 2-2 or
2-2 + Bo-Bo + Bo-Bo + 2-2 + Bo-Bo + Bo-Bo + Bo-Bo + 2-2.
Braking: Disc & regenerative.   **Dimensions:** 26.0 m x 2.7 m.
Bogies: Hitachi.   **Couplers:** Dellner 10.
Gangways: Within unit.   **Control System:** IGBT Inverter.
Doors: Single-leaf sliding.   **Maximum Speed:** 125 mph.
Heating & ventilation: Air conditioning.
Seating Layout: 1: 2+1 facing/unidirectional; 2+2 facing/unidirectional.
Multiple Working: Within class and with Class 801.

Class 800/0. 5-car units for Great Western Railway as replacements for
HSTs. Full details awaited.

DTSO. Hitachi Newton Aycliffe/Kasado 2013–18. –/56 1TD   t.
MSO. Hitachi Newton Aycliffe/Kasado 2013–18. –/88.   t.
MSO. Hitachi Newton Aycliffe/Kasado 2013–18. –/88 2T.   t.
MCO. Hitachi Newton Aycliffe/Kasado 2013–18. 18/58 1T.   t.
DTRBFO. Hitachi Newton Aycliffe/Kasado 2013–18. 18/– 1TD 2W.   t.

800 001		NP	811001	812001	813001	814001	815001
800 002		NP	811002	812002	813002	814002	815002
800 003			811003	812003	813003	814003	815003
800 004	GW	NP	811004	812004	813004	814004	815004
800 005			811005	812005	813005	814005	815005
800 006			811006	812006	813006	814006	815006
800 007			811007	812007	813007	814007	815007
800 008			811008	812008	813008	814008	815008
800 009			811009	812009	813009	814009	815009
800 010			811010	812010	813010	814010	815010
800 011			811011	812011	813011	814011	815011
800 012			811012	812012	813012	814012	815012
800 013			811013	812013	813013	814013	815013
800 014			811014	812014	813014	814014	815014
800 015			811015	812015	813015	814015	815015
800 016			811016	812016	813016	814016	815016
800 017			811017	812017	813017	814017	815017
800 018			811018	812018	813018	814018	815018
800 019			811019	812019	813019	814019	815019
800 020			811020	812020	813020	814020	815020
800 021			811021	812021	813021	814021	815021
800 022			811022	812022	813022	814022	815022
800 023			811023	812023	813023	814023	815023
800 024			811024	812024	813024	814024	815024
800 025			811025	812025	813025	814025	815025
800 026			811026	812026	813026	814026	815026
800 027			811027	812027	813027	814027	815027
800 028			811028	812028	813028	814028	815028
800 029			811029	812029	813029	814029	815029
800 030			811030	812030	813030	814030	815030
800 031			811031	812031	813031	814031	815031
800 032			811032	812032	813032	814032	815032
800 033			811033	812033	813033	814033	815033

800034		811034	812034	813034	814034	815034
800035		811035	812035	813035	814035	815035
800036		811036	812036	813036	814036	815036

Name: 800004   Isambard Kingdom Brunel/Sir Daniel Gooch (carried on alternative driving cars)

Class 800/1. 9-car units for Virgin Trains East Coast as replacements for HSTs. Full details awaited.

DTRBFO. Hitachi Newton Aycliffe/Kasado 2013–18.   t.
MFO. Hitachi Newton Aycliffe/Kasado 2013–18.   t.
MCO. Hitachi Newton Aycliffe/Kasado 2013–18.   t.
TSO. Hitachi Newton Aycliffe/Kasado 2013–18.   t.
MSO. Hitachi Newton Aycliffe/Kasado 2013–18.   t.
MSO. Hitachi Newton Aycliffe/Kasado 2013–18.   t.
MSO. Hitachi Newton Aycliffe/Kasado 2013–18.   t.
MSO. Hitachi Newton Aycliffe/Kasado 2013–18.   t.
DTSO. Hitachi Newton Aycliffe/Kasado 2013–18.   t.

800101	NP	811101	812101	813101	814101	815101
		816101	817101	818101	819101	
800102		811102	812102	813102	814102	815102
		816102	817102	818102	819102	
800103		811103	812103	813103	814103	815103
		816103	817103	818103	819103	
800104		811104	812104	813104	814104	815104
		816104	817104	818104	819104	
800105		811105	812105	813105	814105	815105
		816105	817105	818105	819105	
800106		811106	812106	813106	814106	815106
		816106	817106	818106	819106	
800107		811107	812107	813107	814107	815107
		816107	817107	818107	819107	
800108		811108	812108	813108	814108	815108
		816108	817108	818108	819108	
800109		811109	812109	813109	814109	815109
		816109	817109	818109	819109	
800110		811110	812110	813110	814110	815110
		816110	817110	818110	819110	
800111		811111	812111	813111	814111	815111
		816111	817111	818111	819111	
800112		811112	812112	813112	814112	815112
		816112	817112	818112	819112	
800113		811113	812113	813113	814113	815113
		816113	817113	818113	819113	

Class 800/2. 5-car units for Virgin Trains East Coast as replacements for HSTs. Full details awaited.

DTRBFO. Hitachi Newton Aycliffe/Kasado 2016–18.   t.
MCO. Hitachi Newton Aycliffe/Kasado 2016–18.   t.
MSO. Hitachi Newton Aycliffe/Kasado 2016–18.   t.

MSO. Hitachi Newton Aycliffe/Kasado 2016–18.   t.
DTSO. Hitachi Newton Aycliffe/Kasado 2016–18.   t.

800 201	811201	812201	813201	814201	815201
800 202	811202	812202	813202	814202	815202
800 203	811203	812203	813203	814203	815203
800 204	811204	812204	813204	814204	815204
800 205	811205	812205	813205	814205	815205
800 206	811206	812206	813206	814206	815206
800 207	811207	812207	813207	814207	815207
800 208	811208	812208	813208	814208	815208
800 209	811209	812209	813209	814209	815209
800 210	811210	812210	813210	814210	815210

Class 801/3. 9-car units for Great Western Railway as replacements for HSTs. Originally to be built as full electric trains and numbered in the Class 801/0 series. Full details awaited.

DTRBFO. Hitachi Newton Aycliffe/Kasado 2016–18. 15/– 1TD 2W.   t.
MFO. Hitachi Newton Aycliffe/Kasado 2016–18. 56/– 1T.   t.
MSO. Hitachi Newton Aycliffe/Kasado 2016–18. –/88.   t.
MSO. Hitachi Newton Aycliffe/Kasado 2016–18. –/88 2T.   t.
MSO. Hitachi Newton Aycliffe/Kasado 2016–18. –/88 2T.   t.
MSO. Hitachi Newton Aycliffe/Kasado 2016–18. –/88.   t.
MSO. Hitachi Newton Aycliffe/Kasado 2016–18. –/88 2T.   t.
MSO. Hitachi Newton Aycliffe/Kasado 2016–18. –/88 1T.   t.
DTSO. Hitachi Newton Aycliffe/Kasado 2016–18. –/48 1TD 2W.   t.

800 301	821001	822001	823001	824001	825001
	826001	827001	828001	829001	
800 302	821002	822002	823002	824002	825002
	826002	827002	828002	829002	
800 303	821003	822003	823003	824003	825003
	826003	827003	828003	829003	
800 304	821004	822004	823004	824004	825004
	826004	827004	828004	829004	
800 305	821005	822005	823005	824005	825005
	826005	827005	828005	829005	
800 306	821006	822006	823006	824006	825006
	826006	827006	828006	829006	
800 307	821007	822007	823007	824007	825007
	826007	827007	828007	829007	
800 308	821008	822008	823008	824008	825008
	826008	827008	828008	829008	
800 309	821009	822009	823009	824009	825009
	826009	827009	828009	829009	
800 310	821010	822010	823010	824010	825010
	826010	827010	828010	829010	
800 311	821011	822011	823011	824011	825011
	826011	827011	828011	829011	
800 312	821012	822012	823012	824012	825012
	826012	827012	828012	829012	

800313					
	821013	822013	823013	824013	825013
	826013	827013	828013	829013	
800314	821014	822014	823014	824014	825014
	826014	827014	828014	829014	
800315	821015	822015	823015	824015	825015
	826015	827015	828015	829015	
800316	821016	822016	823016	824016	825016
	826016	827016	828016	829016	
800317	821017	822017	823017	824017	825017
	826017	827017	828017	829017	
800318	821018	822018	823018	824018	825018
	826018	827018	828018	829018	
800319	821019	822019	823019	824019	825019
	826019	827019	828019	829019	
800320	821020	822020	823020	824020	825020
	826020	827020	828020	829020	
800321	821021	822021	823021	824021	825021
	826021	827021	828021	829021	

CLASS 801 INTERCITY EXPRESS PROGRAMME
ELECTRIC   HITACHI

The Class 801s are EMUs, but will still have one diesel engine fitted per unit for emergency use.

Formations: Various, see class headings for details.
Systems: 25 kV AC overhead electric, plus one diesel engine per set.
Construction: Aluminium.
Engines: MTU 12V 1600 R80L of 700 kW (940 hp).
Traction Motors: Four Hitachi asynchronous of 226 kW.
Wheel Arrangement:
Braking: Disc & regenerative.
Bogies: Hitachi.
Gangways: Within unit.
Doors: Single-leaf sliding.
Heating & ventilation: Air conditioning.
Dimensions: 26.0 m x 2.7 m.
Couplers: Dellner 10.
Control System: IGBT Inverter.
Maximum Speed: 125 mph.
Seating Layout: 1: 2+1 facing/unidirectional; 2+2 facing/unidirectional.
Multiple Working: Within class and with Class 800.

Class 801/1. 5-car units for Virgin Trains East Coast as replacements for HSTs. Full details awaited.

DTRBFO. Hitachi Newton Aycliffe/Kasado 2016–18.   t.
MCO. Hitachi Newton Aycliffe/Kasado 2016–18.   t.
MSO. Hitachi Newton Aycliffe/Kasado 2016–18.   t.
MSO. Hitachi Newton Aycliffe/Kasado 2016–18.   t.
DTSO. Hitachi Newton Aycliffe/Kasado 2016–18.   t.

801101	821101	822101	823101	824101	825101
801102	821102	822102	823102	824102	825102
801103	821103	822103	823103	824103	825103

801 104	821104	822104	823104	824104	825104
801 105	821105	822105	823105	824105	825105
801 106	821106	822106	823106	824106	825106
801 107	821107	822107	823107	824107	825107
801 108	821108	822108	823108	824108	825108
801 109	821109	822109	823109	824109	825109
801 110	821110	822110	823110	824110	825110
801 111	821111	822111	823111	824111	825111
801 112	821112	822112	823112	824112	825112

Class 801/2. 9-car units for Virgin Trains East Coast as replacements for locomotive-hauled Class 91+Mark 4 stock. Full details awaited.

DTRBFO. Hitachi Newton Aycliffe 2017–19.   t.
MFO. Hitachi Newton Aycliffe 2017–19.   t.
MCO. Hitachi Newton Aycliffe 2017–19.   t.
MSO. Hitachi Newton Aycliffe 2017–19.   t.
MSO. Hitachi Newton Aycliffe 2017–19.   t.
MSO. Hitachi Newton Aycliffe 2017–19.   t.
MSO. Hitachi Newton Aycliffe 2017–19.   t.
MSO. Hitachi Newton Aycliffe 2017–19.   t.
DTSO. Hitachi Newton Aycliffe 2017–19.   t.

801 201	821201	822201	823201	824201	825201
	826201	827201	828201	829201	
801 202	821202	822202	823202	824202	825202
	826202	827202	828202	829202	
801 203	821203	822203	823203	824203	825203
	826203	827203	828203	829203	
801 204	821204	822204	823204	824204	825204
	826204	827204	828204	829204	
801 205	821205	822205	823205	824205	825205
	826205	827205	828205	829205	
801 206	821206	822206	823206	824206	825206
	826206	827206	828206	829206	
801 207	821207	822207	823207	824207	825207
	826207	827207	828207	829207	
801 208	821208	822208	823208	824208	825208
	826208	827208	828208	829208	
801 209	821209	822209	823209	824209	825209
	826209	827209	828209	829209	
801 210	821210	822210	823210	824210	825210
	826210	827210	828210	829210	
801 211	821211	822211	823211	824211	825211
	826211	827211	828211	829211	
801 212	821212	822212	823212	824212	825212
	826212	827212	828212	829212	
801 213	821213	822213	823213	824213	825213
	826213	827213	828213	829213	
801 214	821214	822214	823214	824214	825214
	826214	827214	828214	829214	

801215	821215	822215	823215	824215	825215
	826215	827215	828215	829215	
801216	821216	822216	823216	824216	825216
	826216	827216	828216	829216	
801217	821217	822217	823217	824217	825217
	826217	827217	828217	829217	
801218	821218	822218	823218	824218	825218
	826218	827218	828218	829218	
801219	821219	822219	823219	824219	825219
	826219	827219	828219	829219	
801220	821220	822220	823220	824220	825220
	826220	827220	828220	829220	
801221	821221	822221	823221	824221	825221
	826221	827221	828221	829221	
801222	821222	822222	823222	824222	825222
	826222	827222	828222	829222	
801223	821223	822223	823223	824223	825223
	826223	827223	828223	829223	
801224	821224	822224	823224	824224	825224
	826224	827224	828224	829224	
801225	821225	822225	823225	824225	825225
	826225	827225	828225	829225	
801226	821226	822226	823226	824226	825226
	826226	827226	828226	829226	
801227	821227	822227	823227	824227	825227
	826227	827227	828227	829227	
801228	821228	822228	823228	824228	825228
	826228	827228	828228	829228	
801229	821229	822229	823229	824229	825229
	826229	827229	828229	829229	
801230	821230	822230	823230	824230	825230
	826230	827230	828230	829230	

5. EUROSTAR UNITS

The original Eurostar Class 373 units were built for and are normally used on services between Britain and continental Europe via the Channel Tunnel. SNCF-owned units 3203/04, 3225/26 and 3227/28 have been removed from the Eurostar pool and were used on Paris–Lille services, but have now been withdrawn. As they are not now permitted through the Channel Tunnel they are not listed here. However the trailers from 3203/04 have now been refurbished to run with power cars 3211/12.

Each Class 373 train consists of two 10-car units coupled, with a motor car at each driving end. All units are articulated with an extra motor bogie on the coach adjacent to the motor car.

All Class 373 sets can be used between London St Pancras and Paris, Brussels and Disneyland Paris. Certain sets (shown *) are equipped for 1500 V DC operation and are used for the winter service to Bourg Saint Maurice and the summer service to Avignon. All eight units being refurbished will be fitted for operation on 1500 V DC.

Seven 8-car Class 373 sets were built for Regional Eurostar services, but all except one power car (3308) and one half set were on long-term hire to SNCF for use on French internal services so are not listed here. They have now been taken out of traffic. Power car 3308 has been preserved at the National Railway Museum, York.

The second generation Eurostar trains, the Siemens Class 374s, are currently being introduced and have already replaced most of the Class 373s, with sets due to start to be scrapped in late 2016. Eight sets are being fully refurbished and retained by Eurostar – 3007/08, 3015/16, 3205/06, 3209/10, 3211/12, 3219/20, 3221/22 and 3229/30.

CLASS 373   "THREE CAPITALS" EUROSTARS

10-car half-sets. Built for services starting from or terminating in London Waterloo (now St Pancras). Individual vehicles in each set are allocated numbers 373xxx0 + 373xxx1 + 373xxx2 + 373xxx3 + 373xxx4 + 373xxx5 + 373xxx6 + 373xxx7 + 373xxx8 + 373xxx9, where 3xxx denotes the set number.

Formation: DM–MSO–4TSO–RB–2TFO–TBFO. Gangwayed within pair of units. Air conditioned.
Construction: Steel.
Supply Systems: 25 kV AC 50 Hz overhead or 3000 V DC overhead (* also equipped for 1500 V DC overhead operation).
Control System: GTO–GTO Inverter on UK 750 V DC and 25 kV AC, GTO Chopper on SNCB 3000 V DC.
Wheel Arrangement: Bo-Bo + Bo–2–2–2–2–2–2–2–2–2.
Lengths: 22.15 m (DM), 21.85 m (MSO & TBFO), 18.70 m (other cars).
Couplers: Schaku 10S at outer ends, Schaku 10L at inner end of each DM and outer ends of each sub set.
Maximum Speed: 186 mph (300 km/h).
Built: 1992–93 by GEC-Alsthom/Brush/ANF/De Dietrich/BN Construction/ACEC.

DM vehicles carry the set numbers indicated below.

† Refurbished (full details awaited).

373xxx0 series. DM. Lot No. 31118 1992–95. 68.5 t.
373xxx1 series. MSO. Lot No. 31119 1992–95. –/48 2T. 44.6 t.
373xxx2 series. TSO. Lot No. 31120 1992–95. –/56 1T. 28.1 t.
373xxx3 series. TSO. Lot No. 31121 1992–95. –/56 2T. 29.7 t.
373xxx4 series. TSO. Lot No. 31122 1992–95. –/56 1T. 28.3 t.
373xxx5 series. TSO. Lot No. 31123 1992–95. –/56 2T. 29.2 t.
373xxx6 series. RB. Lot No. 31124 1992–95. 31.1 t.
373xxx7 series. TFO. Lot No. 31125 1992–95. 39/– 1T. 29.6 t.
373xxx8 series. TFO. Lot No. 31126 1992–95. 39/– 1T. 32.2 t.
373xxx9 series. TBFO. Lot No. 31127 1992–95. 25/– 1TD. 39.4 t.

3001		**EU**	EU	*EU*	TI	3107		**EU**	SB	*EU*	FF
3002		**EU**	EU	*EU*	TI	3108		**EU**	SB	*EU*	FF
3003		**EU**	EU	*EU*	TI	3201	*	**EU**	SF	*EU*	LY
3004		**EU**	EU	*EU*	TI	3202	*	**EU**	SF	*EU*	LY
3005		**EU**	EU	*EU*	TI	3205		**EU**	SF	*EU*	LY
3006		**EU**	EU	*EU*	TI	3206		**EU**	SF	*EU*	LY
3007	*	**ER**	EU	*EU*	TI	3207	*	**EU**	SF		LY (S)
3008	*	**ER**	EU	*EU*	TI	3208	*	**EU**	SF		LY (S)
3009		**EU**	EU	*EU*	TI	3209	*	**EU**	SF	*EU*	LY
3010		**EU**	EU	*EU*	TI	3210	*	**EU**	SF	*EU*	LY
3011		**EU**	EU	*EU*	TI	3211	*	**ER**	SF	*EU*	LY
3012		**EU**	EU	*EU*	TI	3212	*	**ER**	SF	*EU*	LY
3013		**EU**	EU		TI (S)	3213	*	**EU**	SF	*EU*	LY
3014		**EU**	EU		TI (S)	3214	*	**EU**	SF	*EU*	LY
3015	†*	**ER**	EU	*EU*	TI	3215	*	**EU**	SF	*EU*	LY
3016	†*	**ER**	EU	*EU*	TI	3216	*	**EU**	SF	*EU*	LY
3017		**EU**	EU		TI (S)	3217		**EU**	SF	*EU*	LY
3018		**EU**	EU		TI (S)	3218		**EU**	SF	*EU*	LY
3019		**EU**	EU		TI (S)	3219		**ER**	SF	*EU*	LY
3020		**EU**	EU		TI (S)	3220		**ER**	SF	*EU*	LY
3021		**EU**	EU	*EU*	TI	3221		**EU**	SF	*EU*	LY
3022		**EU**	EU	*EU*	TI	3222		**EU**	SF	*EU*	LY
3101		**EU**	SB		TI (S)	3223	*	**EU**	SF	*EU*	LY
3102		**EU**	SB		TI (S)	3224	*	**EU**	SF	*EU*	LY
3103		**EU**	SB	*EU*	FF	3229	*	**EU**	SF	*EU*	LY
3104		**EU**	SB	*EU*	FF	3230	*	**EU**	SF	*EU*	LY
3105		**EU**	SB	*EU*	FF	3231		**EU**	SF	*EU*	LY
3106		**EU**	SB	*EU*	FF	3232		**EU**	SF	*EU*	LY

Spare DM:

3999   **ER**   EU   *EU*   TI

Names:

3001/02	Tread Lightly/Voyage Vert	3013/14	LONDON 2012
3003/04	Tri-City-Athlon 2010	3207/08	MICHEL HOLLARD
3007/08	Waterloo Sunset	3209/10	THE DA VINCI CODE
3009/10	REMEMBERING FROMELLES		

CLASS 374   SIEMENS VELARO e320

8-car half-sets. Currently being delivered. These units are similar to the DB Class 407 ICE sets, with distributed power rather than a power car at either end like the Class 373s. The first sets entered service in November 2015, operating initially on the St Pancras–Paris route. They will also be used on the proposed St Pancras–Amsterdam service from December 2017.

The initial order was for ten units (4001–20) and this was then increased by another seven (4021–34) in 2014. An option exists for a further six units.

Formation: DMFO–TBFO–MFO–TSO–TSO–MSO–TSO–MSORB.
Gangwayed within pair of units. Air conditioned.
Construction: Aluminium.   **Control System:** IGBT Inverter.
Supply Systems: 25 kV AC 50 Hz overhead, 1500 V DC overhead and 3000 V DC overhead.
Continuous rating: 8000 kW (AC), 4200 kW (DC).
Wheel Arrangement: Bo-Bo + 2-2 + Bo-Bo + 2-2 + 2-2 + Bo-Bo + 2-2 + Bo-Bo.
Lengths: 26.035 m (DMFO), 24.775 m (other cars).
Couplers: Dellner 12.   **Maximum Speed:** 200 mph (320 km/h).
Built: 2012–17 by Siemens, Krefeld, Germany.

DM vehicles carry the full 12-digit EVNs as indicated below. For example set 4001/02 carries the numbers 93 70 3740 011-9 + 93 70 3740 012-7 + 93 70 3740 013-5 + 93 70 3740 014-3 + 93 70 3740 015-0 + 93 70 3740 016-8 + 93 70 3740 017-6 + 93 70 3740 018-4 + 93 70 3740 028-3 + 93 70 3740 027-5 + 93 70 3740 026-7 + 93 70 3740 025-9 + 93 70 3740 024-2 + 93 70 3740 023-4 + 93 70 3740 022-6 + 93 70 3740 021-8.

93 70 3740 xx1-c series. DMFO. Siemens Krefeld 2012–17. 40/–. 58.0 t.
93 70 3740 xx2-c series. TBFO. Siemens Krefeld 2012–17. 36/– 2T. 59.0 t.
93 70 3740 xx3-c series. MFO. Siemens Krefeld 2012–17. 34/–(+2) 1TD 2W. 59.0 t.
93 70 3740 xx4-c series. TSO. Siemens Krefeld 2012–17. –/76 2T. 53.0 t.
93 70 3740 xx5-c series. TSO. Siemens Krefeld 2012–17. –/76 2T. 53.0 t.
93 70 3740 xx6-c series. MSO. Siemens Krefeld 2012–17. –/76 2T. 58.0 t.
93 70 3740 xx7-c series. TSO. Siemens Krefeld 2012–17. –/76 2T. 57.0 t.
93 70 3740 xx8-c series. MSORB. Siemens Krefeld 2012–17. –/32 2T. 58.0 t.

4001	**ER**	EU	*EU*	TI		4018	**ER**	EU	*EU*	TI
4002	**ER**	EU	*EU*	TI		4019	**ER**	EU	*EU*	TI
4003	**ER**	EU	*EU*	TI		4020	**ER**	EU	*EU*	TI
4004	**ER**	EU	*EU*	TI		4021	**ER**	EU	*EU*	TI
4005	**ER**	EU	*EU*	TI		4022	**ER**	EU	*EU*	TI
4006	**ER**	EU	*EU*	TI		4023	**ER**	EU
4007	**ER**	EU	*EU*	TI		4024	**ER**	EU
4008	**ER**	EU	*EU*	TI		4025	**ER**	EU
4009	**ER**	EU	*EU*	TI		4026	**ER**	EU
4010	**ER**	EU	*EU*	TI		4027	**ER**	EU
4011	**ER**	EU	*EU*	TI		4028	**ER**	EU
4012	**ER**	EU	*EU*	TI		4029	**ER**	EU
4013	**ER**	EU	*EU*	TI		4030	**ER**	EU
4014	**ER**	EU	*EU*	TI		4031	**ER**	EU
4015	**ER**	EU	*EU*	TI		4032	**ER**	EU
4016	**ER**	EU	*EU*	TI		4033	**ER**	EU
4017	**ER**	EU	*EU*	TI		4034	**ER**	EU

6. SERVICE EMUS

The following unit is used by Network Rail for ERTMS testing on the Hertford Loop. It has been heavily modified from its original condition, and now includes a toilet.

313121 **Y** BN *GB* WN 62549 71233 62613

7. EMU VEHICLES IN INDUSTRIAL SERVICE

This list comprises EMU vehicles that have been withdrawn from active service but continue to be used in industrial service.

Cl. 390	69133	69833		Virgin Trains Training Centre, Westmere Drive, Crewe, Cheshire
Cl. 390	69633	69733		The Fire Service College, Moreton-in-Marsh, Gloucestershire
Cl. 390	69933			Safety & Accident Investigation Centre, Cranfield University, Cranfield, Bedfordshire
Cl. 508	64649	64712		Emergency Services Training Centre, Seacombe, Merseyside
Cl. 508	64681	71511	64724	The Fire Service College, Moreton-in-Marsh, Gloucestershire

8. EMUS AWAITING DISPOSAL

This list comprises vehicles awaiting disposal which are stored on the national railway network.

25 kV AC 50 Hz OVERHEAD UNITS:

Cl. 309	**RR**	WC	CS	71758
Cl. 365	**N**	X	ZN	65919

750 V DC THIRD RAIL UNITS:

Cl. 508	**CN**	A	ZG	64680	64723

9. CODES

9.1. LIVERY CODES

AL Advertising/promotional livery (see class heading for details).
CN Connex/Southeastern (white with black window surrounds & grey lower band).
ER Revised Eurostar (deep blue & two-tone grey).
EU Eurostar (white with dark blue & yellow stripes).
FB First Group dark blue.
FT First TransPennine Express "Dynamic Lines" (varying blue with multi-coloured lines).
FU First Group "Urban Lights" (varying blue or uniform indigo blue with pink, white & blue markings on the lower bodyside).
GA Abellio Greater Anglia (white with red doors & black window surrounds).
GV Gatwick Express Class 442 (red, white & indigo blue with mauve & blue doors).
GW Great Western Railway (TOC) dark green.
GX Gatwick Express Class 387 (red with white lining and grey doors).
HC Heathrow Connect (grey with a broad deep blue bodyside band & orange doors).
HE Heathrow Express (silver with purple doors and black window surrounds). Red advertising for Vodaphone.
LM London Midland (grey & green with black stripe around the windows).
LO London Overground (all over white with a blue solebar, black window surrounds and orange doors).
LT London Transport maroon & cream.
MY Merseyrail (all over yellow or all over grey (alternate sides)).
N BR Network SouthEast (white & blue with red lower bodyside stripe, grey solebar & cab ends).
NB Northern all over dark blue.
NC National Express white (white with blue doors).
NO Northern (deep blue, purple & white).
NP Northern Electrics purple (all over purple with dark blue ends and doors).
NX National Express (white with grey ends).
O Non-standard (see class heading for details).
RL Royal Mail revised (all over red).
RM Royal Mail (red with yellow stripes above solebar).
RR Regional Railways (dark blue/grey with light blue & white stripes, three narrow dark blue stripes at cab ends).
SB Southeastern blue (all over blue with black window surrounds).
SC Strathclyde PTE (carmine & cream lined out in black & gold).
SD South West Trains outer suburban livery {Class 450 style} (deep blue with red doors & orange & red cab sides).
SE Southeastern suburban (all over white with black window surrounds, light blue doors and (on some units) dark blue lower bodyside stripe).
SN Southern (white & dark green with light green semi-circles at one end of each vehicle. Light grey band at solebar level).
SR ScotRail – Scotland's Railways (dark blue with Scottish Saltire flag & white/light blue flashes).

SS South West Trains inner suburban {Class 455 style} (red with blue & orange flashes at unit ends).

ST Stagecoach {long-distance stock} (white & dark blue with dark blue window surrounds and red & orange swishes at unit ends).

TG Govia Thameslink interim {Class 387} (white with dark green doors}.

TL Govia Thameslink Railway (light grey & white with light blue doors).

VT Virgin Trains silver (silver, with black window surrounds, white cantrail stripe and red roof. Red swept down at unit ends).

XR TfL Crossrail (white with blue doors and lower bodyside stripe).

Y Network Rail yellow.

YR West Yorkshire PTE/Northern EMUs (red, lilac & grey).

9.2. OWNER CODES

A   Angel Trains
CL   Cross London Trains
E   Eversholt Rail (UK)
EU   Eurostar (UK)
HE   Heathrow Airport Holdings
MQ Macquarie Group
P   Porterbrook Leasing Company
PC   Pamplona Capital Management
QW QW Rail Leasing
RM Royal Mail
SB   SNCB/NMBS (Société Nationale des Chemins de fer Belges Nationale Maatschappij der Belgische Spoorwegen)
SF   SNCF (Société Nationale des Chemins de fer Français)
SW South West Trains
WC West Coast Railway Company

9.3. OPERATOR CODES

C2 c2c
DB DB Cargo
EU Eurostar (UK)
GA Abellio Greater Anglia
GN Great Northern (part of Govia Thameslink Railway)
HC Heathrow Connect
HE Heathrow Express
LM London Midland
LO London Overground
ME Merseyrail
NO Northern
SE Southeastern
SN Southern (part of Govia Thameslink Railway)
SR ScotRail
SW South West Trains
TL Thameslink (part of Govia Thameslink Railway)
VW Virgin Trains West Coast
XR Crossrail

9.4. ALLOCATION & LOCATION CODES

Code	Location	Depot Operator
AD	Ashford (Kent)	Hitachi
AK	Ardwick (Manchester)	Siemens
BD	Birkenhead North	Merseyrail
BF	Bedford Cauldwell Walk	Govia Thameslink Railway
BI	Brighton Lovers Walk	Govia Thameslink Railway
CE	Crewe International	DB Cargo
CS	Carnforth	West Coast Railway Company
EM	East Ham (London)	c2c
EP	Ely (Potter Group)	Potter Group Logistics
FF	Forest (Brussels)	SNCB/NMBS
GW	Glasgow Shields Road	ScotRail
HE	Hornsey (London)	Govia Thameslink Railway
IL	Ilford (London)	Abellio Greater Anglia
LB	Loughborough Works	Brush Traction
LG	Longsight (Manchester)	Northern
LY	Le Landy (Paris)	SNCF
MA	Manchester Longsight	Alstom
NG	New Cross Gate (London)	London Overground
NL	Neville Hill (Leeds)	East Midlands Trains/Northern
NN	Northampton King's Heath	Siemens
NP	North Pole (London)	Hitachi
NT	Northam (Southampton)	Siemens
OH	Old Oak Common Heathrow (London)	Heathrow Express
RG	Reading	Great Western Railway
RM	Ramsgate	Southeastern
RY	Ryde (Isle of Wight)	South West Trains
SG	Slade Green (London)	Southeastern
SL	Stewarts Lane (London)	Govia Thameslink Railway/Belmond
SO	Soho (Birmingham)	London Midland
SU	Selhurst (Croydon)	Govia Thameslink Railway
TB	Three Bridges (Crawley)	Siemens
TI	Temple Mills (London)	Eurostar
WB	Wembley (London)	Alstom
WD	Wimbledon (London)	South West Trains
ZA	RTC Business Park (Derby)	LORAM
ZB	Doncaster Works	Wabtec Rail
ZC	Crewe Works	Bombardier Transportation UK
ZD	Derby Works	Bombardier Transportation UK
ZG	Eastleigh Works	Arlington Fleet Services
ZH	Springburn Depot (Glasgow)	Knorr-Bremse Rail Systems (UK)
ZI	Ilford Works	Bombardier Transportation UK
ZJ	Stoke-on-Trent Works	Axiom Rail (Stoke)
ZK	Kilmarnock Works	Wabtec Rail Scotland
ZN	Wolverton Works	Knorr-Bremse Rail Systems (UK)
ZR	York (Holgate Works)	Network Rail